EUREKA!

CRITICAL READING SERIES

¡EUREKA!

21 Stories of Momentous Discoveries and Inventions—with Exercises for Developing Reading Comprehension and Critical Thinking Skills

Henry Billings

Melissa Billings

JAMESTOWN PUBLISHERS

a division of NTC/CONTEMPORARY PUBLISHING GROUP
Lincolnwood, Illinois USA

ISBN 0-89061-249-8

Published by Jamestown Publishers,
a division of NTC/Contemporary Publishing Group, Inc.
4255 West Touhy Avenue
Lincolnwood (Chicago), Illinois 60646-1975, U.S.A.
9 0 VL 0 9 8 7 6 5 4 3 2 1

CONTENTS

To the Student

Archimedes was a scientist and inventor in ancient Greece. According to an old story, King Hiero went to Archimedes for help when he had a puzzling problem. The king suspected that the goldsmith who made his crown had not used pure gold, but had secretly mixed the gold with a cheaper metal. King Hiero asked Archimedes to figure out a way to prove whether or not the crown was solid gold.

Archimedes thought long and hard about the problem but could not come up with a solution. Then, the story says, while Archimedes was in his bathtub, the answer suddenly came to him. He noticed that water ran out of the tub when he placed his body into it. The more room an object takes up, Archimedes reasoned, the more water it pushes out, or displaces. He immediately understood that if he placed both the crown and the same weight of pure gold into the water, each object should displace the same amount of water, that is, if they are both solid gold. Archimedes was so excited with his discovery that he dashed out into the street shouting, "Eureka!" which means "I have found it!" As it turned out, when Archimedes finally did his experiment, he found that the crown displaced more water than an equal weight of pure gold, so the crown was not pure gold. The goldsmith was caught cheating.

Like Archimedes, each of the people you will read about in this book experienced a moment when he or she felt the joy of discovery—a "Eureka!" moment. Each lesson will introduce you to a different person or group of people who invented or discovered something that changed history. Some of these people dedicated their entire lives to the search. Others fell into their discoveries and inventions by chance. All of their stories are spellbinding.

As you read and enjoy the articles in this book, you will also be developing your reading skills. *Eureka!* is for students who already read fairly well but who want to read faster and to increase their understanding of what they read. If you complete the 21 lessons— reading the articles and completing the exercises—you will surely increase your reading speed and improve your reading comprehension and critical thinking skills. Also, because these exercises include items of the types often found on state and national tests, learning how to complete them will prepare you for tests you may have to take in the future.

How to Use This Book

About the Book.   *Eureka!* contains three units, each of which includes seven lessons. Each lesson begins with an article about an unusual event, person, or group. The article is followed by a group of four reading comprehension exercises and a set of three critical thinking exercises. The reading comprehension exercises will help you understand the article. The critical thinking exercises will help you think about what you have read and how it relates to your own experience.

At the end of each lesson, you will also have the opportunity to give your personal response to some aspect of the article and then to assess how well you understood what you read.

The Sample Lesson.   Working through the sample lesson, the first lesson in the book, with your class or group will demonstrate how a lesson is organized. The sample lesson explains how to complete the exercises and score your answers. The correct answers for the sample exercises and sample scores are printed in lighter type. In some cases, explanations of the correct answers are given. The explanations will help you understand how to think through these question types.

If you have any questions about how to complete the exercises or score them, this is the time to get the answers.

Working Through Each Lesson.   Begin each lesson by looking at the photographs and reading the captions. Before you read, predict what you think the article will be about. Then read the article.

Sometimes your teacher may decide to time your reading. Timing helps you keep track of and increase your reading speed. If you have been timed, enter your reading time in the box at the end of the lesson. Then use the Words-per-Minute Table to find your reading speed, and record your speed on the Reading Speed graph at the end of the unit.

Next complete the Reading Comprehension and Critical Thinking exercises. The directions for each exercise will tell you how to mark your answers. When you have finished all four Reading Comprehension exercises, use the answer key provided by your teacher to check your work. Follow the directions after each exercise to find your score. Record your Reading Comprehension scores on the graph at the end of each unit. Then check your answers to the Author's Approach, Summarizing and Paraphrasing, and Critical Thinking exercises. Fill in the Critical Thinking chart at the end of each unit with your evaluation of your work and comments about your progress.

At the end of each unit you will also complete a Compare/Contrast chart. The completed chart will help you see what the articles have in common, and it will give you an opportunity to explore your own opinions about these inventions and discoveries that changed the world.

THE BIRTH OF THE BLUES
(Jeans, That Is)

Nothing is more American than a pair of blue jeans. At one time only Americans wore them. The fashion has long since spread around the world. Still, blue jeans remain a popular symbol of America. They didn't begin as a fashion statement, however. They began as a practical solution to a practical problem.

2   In 1849, gold was discovered in California. That news sparked the famous California Gold Rush. Thousands of "Forty-Niners" rushed to the gold fields hoping to find their fortune. A few miners did strike it rich. But most did not. They spent whatever money they made on lodging, food, clothing, picks, and shovels. Clothing was a particular problem. The miners spent long days kneeling in dirt, scrambling over rocks, and squatting in water. Under these conditions, pants wore out quickly. Miners complained about how easily their pants ripped or the seams pulled out. As one miner put it, "pants don't wear worth a hoot up in the diggin's."

3   According to legend, one miner mentioned this problem to a merchant

A gold miner pans for gold in northern California about 1890. Pants made by Levi Strauss Company were very popular among miners.

named Levi Strauss. Strauss had been born in Germany in 1829. At the age of 17, he came to America and settled in New York City. There he worked in his brother's store selling dry goods such as shirts, blankets, pillows, and underwear. In 1853, Levi Strauss sailed to San Francisco to make his fortune. He planned to make his money not by panning for gold, but by running a store. He figured he could sell all sorts of dry goods to miners. Strauss even brought some canvas with him. He thought the material would make good tents or wagon covers.

4   After hearing the miners' clothing complaints, though, Strauss changed his mind. He used the canvas to make up some pants for miners. Calling them "waist-high overalls," he sold them for 22¢ a pair. The miners loved "those pants of Levi's" or "Levi's" for short. One miner even sat in a watering trough until his Levi's shrank to a perfect fit. The brown pants were homely, but they wore like iron. They were so tough, one story goes, that when a coupling broke between two train cars, the engineer took off his Levi's and tied the cars together with them.

5   Strauss sold his pants as fast as he could make them. Still, he constantly worked to improve his product. He switched from canvas to French denim, a cotton twill material even stronger and more durable than canvas. Later he also changed his dye color to a dark indigo blue. Because of the new color, some people began to call their Levi's "blue denims" or "blue jeans." (The word *jeans* comes from the name of a city in Italy also associated with denim pants—Genoa.)

6   But there was still one major problem with the Levi's. The pants themselves never ripped, but sometimes the seams did. This was especially true in areas of stress such as the pockets. Miners often stuffed samples of ore in their pockets. The pressure frequently ripped open the pockets. In 1872, a tailor named Jacob Davis came up with a brilliant idea. He was tired of sewing up the same pockets over and over again. So Davis put copper rivets on the corners of the pockets and at the base of the fly. It worked. The seams didn't rip anymore.

7   Davis lacked the money to patent his process. So he wrote to Strauss and suggested a partnership. Strauss agreed. A patent for the new process was issued on May 20, 1873. And so the modern blue jean was born. Before long, Levi Strauss & Company became the largest clothing manufacturer in the world.

8   Strauss had intended to make simple work pants. But his blue jeans became immensely popular for all-around use far beyond the gold fields. Men and women in all walks of life enjoyed them. *Vogue* magazine featured women in Levi's as early as 1935. Lana Turner, a famous movie star, had her blue jeans studded with diamonds.

Levi Strauss (above) probably had no idea how his blue jeans would revolutionize fashion in 20th-century America and around the world.

9   The rivets on the rear pockets, though, did not last. When children began wearing blue jeans to school, the rivets scratched the school chairs and desks. Teachers complained. And so in 1937 the rivets on the rear pockets were taken out. They were replaced by extra heavy stitching.

10   Later, blue jeans became a hot item in communist nations. In the old Soviet Union, for instance, they sold for as much as $140 a pair on the black market. In some communist nations, blue jeans were used as a form of money. So it may be that communism fell not because the U.S. had better weapons but because we had better pants!

11   Today Levi's are still one tough pair of pants. Take the case of a construction worker in Fort Worth, Texas. It seems that one day he was working atop a 52-story building. A nearby crane accidentally hooked a pocket of his Levi's and swung him out over the abyss. "I thought I was gone," he later said, "but the hook had me caught so that the Levi's didn't rip until another man…got me to safety." Back on firm ground, the man wrote a heartfelt thank you note to Levi Strauss & Company. ✍

If you have been timed while reading this article, enter your reading time below. Then turn to the Words-per-Minute Table on page 71 and look up your reading speed (words per minute). Enter your reading speed on the graph on page 72.

Reading Time: Sample Lesson

_____ : _____
Minutes   Seconds

A Finding the Main Idea

One statement below expresses the main idea of the article. One statement is too general, or too broad. The other statement explains only part of the article; it is too narrow. Label the statements using the following key:

M—Main Idea   **B—Too Broad**   **N—Too Narrow**

_N_   1. Levi's became so popular around the world that they sometimes sold for as much as $140 in the old Soviet Union. [This statement is true, but it is *too narrow*. It presents only one fact from the article.]

_B_   2. Some items of clothing can be both practical and fashionable. [This statement is true, but it is *too broad*. This article is about a particular item of clothing—blue jeans.]

_M_   3. Blue jeans were created by Levi Strauss to fill the needs of California gold miners and have become popular worldwide. [This statement is the *main idea*. It tells you that the article is about blue jeans and their inventor. It also tells you why they were created.]

_15_   Score 15 points for a correct M answer.

_10_   Score 5 points for each correct B or N answer.

_25_   **Total Score:** Finding the Main Idea

B Recalling Facts

How well do you remember the facts in the article? Put an X in the box next to the answer that correctly completes each statement about the article.

1. Gold was discovered in California in
   ☒ a. 1849.
   ☐ b. 1897.
   ☐ c. 1929.

2. Levi Straus opened his own dry goods store in
   ☐ a. Los Angeles.
   ☒ b. San Francisco.
   ☐ c. New York City.

3. Although Strauss first made his pants from canvas, he soon switched to
   ☐ a. wool.
   ☐ b. linen.
   ☒ c. blue denim.

4. To make the pockets stronger, Jacob Davis
   ☒ a. put copper rivets on the corners of the pockets.
   ☐ b. sewed all the pocket seams twice.
   ☐ c. made them from a stronger material.

5. Levi Strauss and Jacob Davis
   ☐ a. tried to put each other out of business.
   ☐ b. sued one another.
   ☒ c. became partners.

Score 5 points for each correct answer.

_25_   **Total Score:** Recalling Facts

C | Making Inferences

When you combine your own experience and information from a text to draw a conclusion that is not directly stated in that text, you are making an inference. Below are five statements that may or may not be inferences based on information in the article. Label the statements using the following key:

C—Correct Inference   F—Faulty Inference

___C___ 1. Levi Strauss was a good businessman. [This is a *correct* inference. The article mentions that Strauss listened to customers and worked hard to fill their needs.]

___F___ 2. Strauss's main goal in changing his pants was to make them more stylish. [This is a *faulty* inference. The article says that the new material was stronger and more durable. It doesn't mention his desire to be fashionable.]

___C___ 3. Many people wear blue jeans because these pants look good and feel good on them. [This is a *correct* inference. The article says that blue jeans have become very popular with all types of people. It mentions that fashion models and movie stars wear them.]

___F___ 4. Obtaining a patent for an invention is free. [This is a *faulty* inference. The article states that Jacob Davis couldn't afford to patent his copper riveting process. It follows that a patent is not free.]

___F___ 5. Workers no longer wear Levi's on the job. [This is a *faulty* inference. The article mentions a construction worker who was recently involved in an accident in which his Levi's came in handy.]

Score 5 points for each correct answer.

___25___ **Total Score:** Making Inferences

D | Using Words Precisely

Each numbered sentence below contains an underlined word or phrase from the article. Following the sentence are three definitions. One definition is closest to the meaning of the underlined word. One definition is opposite or nearly opposite. Label those two definitions using the following key. Do not label the remaining definition.

C—Closest   O—Opposite or Nearly Opposite

1. The brown pants were <u>homely</u>, but they wore like iron.

   _____ a. large

   ___C___ b. ugly

   ___O___ c. beautiful

2. But his blue jeans became <u>immensely</u> popular for all-around use far beyond the gold fields.

   _____ a. fortunately

   ___C___ b. extremely

   ___O___ c. barely

3. Lana Turner, a famous movie star, had her blue jeans <u>studded</u> with diamonds.

   ___C___ a. decorated

   _____ b. shortened

   ___O___ c. stripped or made bare

4. A nearby crane accidentally hooked a pocket of his Levi's and swung him out over the <u>abyss</u>.

   ___O___ a. an extremely high land feature

   ___C___ b. a very deep space

   _____ c. a frightening area

5. Back on firm ground, the man wrote a <u>heartfelt</u> thank you note to Levi Strauss & Company.

_____0_____ a. cynical

_____ b. simple

_____C_____ c. sincere

_____15_____ Score 3 points for each correct C answer.

_____10_____ Score 2 points for each correct O answer.

_____25_____ **Total Score:** Using Words Precisely

Enter the four total scores in the spaces below, and add them together to find your Reading Comprehension Score. Then record your score on the graph on page 73.

Score	Question Type	Sample Lesson
25	Finding the Main Idea	
25	Recalling Facts	
25	Making Inferences	
25	Using Words Precisely	
100	**Reading Comprehension Score**	

Author's Approach

Put an X in the box next to the correct answer.

1. The main purpose of the first paragraph is to

☒ a. introduce the reader to the topic of the article.

☐ b. explain how Levi Strauss invented blue jeans.

☐ c. describe the first blue jeans.

2. From the statements below, choose those that you believe the author would agree with.

☐ a. As a boy, Levi Strauss always dreamed of designing clothing.

☒ b. Levi Strauss didn't expect his pants to be worn by fashion models.

☐ c. Levi Strauss sold his pants for more than they were worth.

3. What does the author mean by the statement "The pants were homely, but they wore like iron"?

☐ a. The pants were so ugly that no one wanted to wear them outside his or her home.

☐ b. The pants were very stiff and uncomfortable.

☒ c. Even though the pants weren't attractive, people liked them because they were so strong.

4. The author tells this story mainly by

☒ a. describing events in the order they happened.

☐ b. comparing different topics.

☐ c. using his or her imagination and creativity.

_____4_____ Number of correct answers

Record your personal assessment of your work on the Critical Thinking Chart on page 74.

Summarizing and Paraphrasing

Put an X in the box next to the correct answer.

1. Below are summaries of the article. Choose the summary that says all the most important things about the article but in the fewest words.

☐ a. Blue jeans are popular all over the world. [This summary leaves out almost all of the important details, such as how blue jeans were invented and why people like to wear them.]

☐ b. When blue jeans were first invented by Levi Strauss to fill the needs of "Forty-Niners" who were looking for gold in California, they were made out of canvas. Soon Strauss made them from blue denim, and Jacob Davis thought of a way to strengthen their pocket seams with copper riveting. Today people still like to wear Levi's on the job and at play. [This summary presents all of the important ideas from the article but includes too many unnecessary details.]

☒ c. Blue jeans, first made by Levi Strauss for "Forty-Niners," have undergone changes over the years, but they are still popular and practical. [This summary says all the most important things about the article in the fewest words.]

2. Read the statement about the article below. Then read the paraphrase of that statement. Choose the reason that best tells why the paraphrase does not say the same thing as the statement.

Statement: When Levi Strauss came west, he brought along some canvas to use in making tents and wagon covers.

Paraphrase: Levi Strauss carried canvas to his new home in the west, hoping that he could use it to make his new pants.

☐ a. Paraphrase says too much.

☐ b. Paraphrase doesn't say enough.

☒ c. Paraphrase doesn't agree with the statement about the article. [The first statement explains that Strauss planned to make tents and wagon covers from canvas, while the paraphrase states that Strauss intended all along to make pants with the material.]

___2___ Number of correct answers

Record your personal assessment of your work on the Critical Thinking Chart on page 74.

Critical Thinking

Follow the directions provided for questions 1 and 3. Put an X in the box next to the correct answer for the other questions.

1. For each statement below, write O if it expresses an opinion or write F if it expresses a fact.

F a. Levi Strauss sold his waist-high overalls for 22¢ a pair.

O b. Blue jeans look old-fashioned today.

F c. Levi Straus was born in Germany.

2. From what the article told about blue jeans, you can predict that

☐ a. manufacturers will soon stop making them.

☐ b. people will soon decide that blue jeans are not comfortable.

☒ c. people will continue to wear them.

3. Choose from the letters below to correctly complete the following statement. Write the letters on the lines.

   On the positive side, ____*a*____, but on the negative side ____*c*____

   a. Levi's canvas pants were strong

   b. Levi's canvas pants were brown

   c. Levi's canvas pants were unattractive

4. What was the cause of the Forty-Niners' dissatisfaction with their pants?

   ☒ a. Their pants ripped too easily.

   ☐ b. Their pants were too expensive.

   ☐ c. Their pants weren't attractive enough.

5. What did you have to do to answer question 2?

   ☐ a. find a cause (why something happened)

   ☐ b. find an opinion (what someone thinks about something)

   ☒ c. make a prediction (what might happen next)

   ____5____ Number of correct answers

   Record your personal assessment of your work on the Critical Thinking Chart on page 74.

Personal Response

Would you recommend this article to other students? Explain.

[Decide whether you'd like to share this article with other

students. Then explain what you liked or disliked about it.]

_____

_____

Self-Assessment

While reading the article, I found it easiest to

[Recall facts about blue jeans or the California Gold Rush that

you knew before you read the article.]

_____

_____

_____

CRITICAL THINKING

Self-Assessment

To get the most out of the Critical Reading series program, you need to take charge of your own progress in improving your reading comprehension and critical thinking skills. Here are some of the features that help you work on those essential skills.

Reading Comprehension Exercises. Complete these exercises immediately after reading the article. They help you recall what you have read, understand the stated and implied main ideas, and add words to your working vocabulary.

Critical Thinking Skills Exercises. These exercises help you focus on the author's approach and purpose, recognize and generate summaries and paraphrases, and identify relationships between ideas.

Personal Response and Self-assessment. Questions in this category help you relate the articles to your personal experience and give you the opportunity to evaluate your understanding of the information in that lesson.

Compare and Contrast Charts. At the end of each unit you will complete a Compare and Contrast chart. The completed chart helps you see what the articles have in common and gives you an opportunity to explore your own ideas about the topics discussed in the articles.

The Graphs. The graphs and charts at the end of each unit enable you to keep track of your progress. Check your graphs regularly with your teacher. Decide whether your progress is satisfactory or whether you need additional work on some skills. What types of exercises are you having difficulty with? Talk with your teacher about ways to work on the skills in which you need the most practice.

UNIT ONE

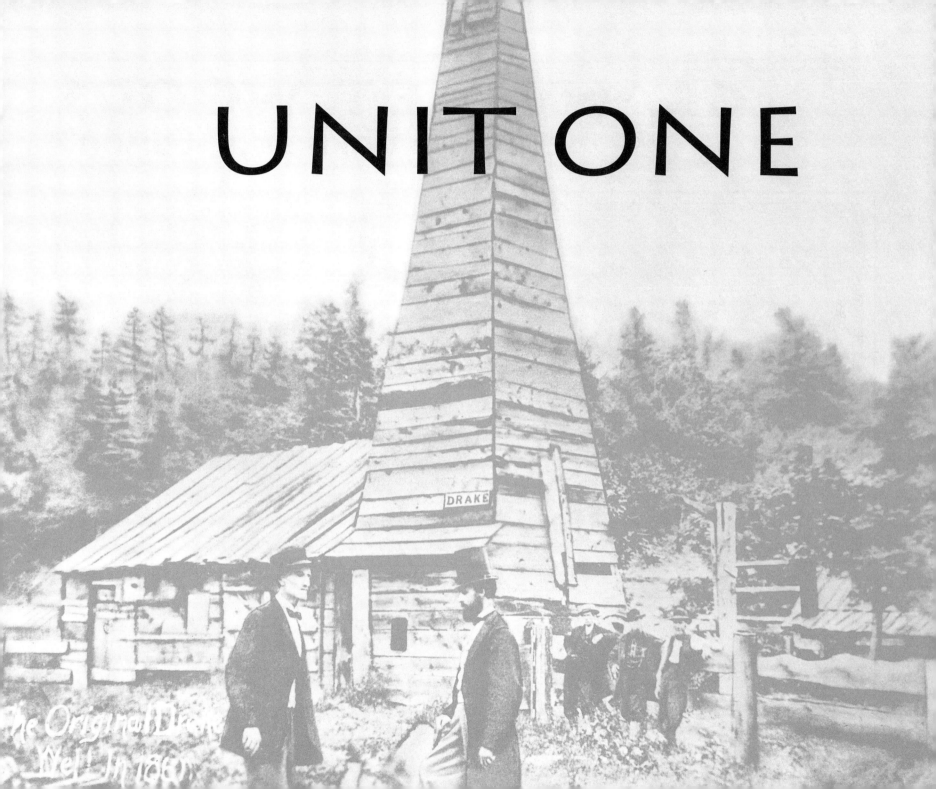

The Original Drake Well in 1860

GRANVILLE T. WOODS
The Unknown "Edison"

Granville T. Woods invented better air brakes for trains. He also invented a telegraph system that enabled moving trains to communicate with each other and avoid accidents.

Granville T. Woods left school at the age of 10. He went to work in an Ohio machine shop. As a free African American in the 1860s, he wasn't paid very much. But every little bit helped his struggling family.

2 Woods quickly picked up the skills needed to be a fine machinist. He also mastered the art of blacksmithing. Wood didn't stop there. He wanted to learn more about all sorts of things. So he began attending night school. He also sought out private teachers who could help him expand his knowledge of the world.

3 Woods was intrigued by machines and engines of all kinds. In his spare time he read many books on engineering and electricity. To get the books, he either borrowed them from friends or had friends check out them of libraries. He couldn't check them out himself. Most libraries at the time wouldn't loan books to blacks. Throughout his life, Woods had to battle racist laws and practices. But he refused to let these obstacles stop him.

4 For several years, Woods bounced from one interesting job to another. In 1872, he

landed a job as a fireman on a railroad. In time, he was promoted to engineer. Then, in 1874, Woods moved to Springfield, Illinois, to work in a steel mill. Two years later he went to New York City to work in a machine shop. Later Woods began traveling the world as an engineer aboard a British steamship. Finally he and his brother, Lyates, decided to open their own machine shop in Cincinnati.

5   Here the brilliant Woods began his true career—that of inventor. He used his vast knowledge and creativity to solve some of the most perplexing problems of his time. On January 3, 1884, he received his first U.S. patent. It was for a steam boiler furnace. The furnace burned fuel much more efficiently than older models. Later that year, Woods got his second patent. This one was for a new telephone transmitter. A third patent in 1885 was for a machine that transmitted messages by electricity. In essence, this invention combined the telegraph with the telephone. With the flip of a switch, the same line could carry either Morse Code or the spoken word. Woods sold many of his patent rights to giant corporations such as Bell Telephone and General Electric.

6   In all, Woods received 45 patents from the U.S. Patent Office. One was for an egg incubator. That early incubator led the way to today's modern machines, which can incubate up to 50,000 eggs at a time. Woods designed better air brakes for railroad trains. He also built a safety switch for electric circuits. He invented an amusement park ride. And he came up with a plan for overhead electric lines to power trolleys.

7   Woods invented so many things that some people called him the "black Thomas Edison." Given the scope of Woods's genius, that compliment could have been reversed. Edison might have been called the "white Granville Woods." In 1886, the *Catholic Tribune* wrote, "Granville T. Woods is the greatest [black] inventor in the history of the race...." It said he was "equal, if not superior, to any inventor in the country." The next year, this same paper called Woods "the greatest electrician in the world."

8   In 1887, Woods made his biggest breakthrough of all. It was one of the greatest inventions of the 19th century. Woods came up with something that saved untold lives and prevented countless accidents. He called it the Multiplex Railway Telegraph. Before this invention, moving trains could not get in touch with each other. Conductors had no way of knowing what trains might be in front of them or what trains might be gaining on them from behind. They could not be warned about broken rails or obstacles on the tracks. Riding blind like this caused many train wrecks. It also cost time since conductors were afraid to go very fast.

9   Woods's Multiplex Railway Telegraph allowed conductors to "see" beyond the horizon. It sent out signals from each

Granville T. Woods, known as the black Thomas Edison

train. These signals could be picked up by other trains and by nearby railroad stations. The new system allowed conductors to tell where the other trains were. It also allowed trains to stay in touch with railroad stations. The invention was a big boost for the railroad industry.

10   Other inventors had tried to create similar systems. For example, Thomas Edison had worked on the problem. But it was Woods who first proclaimed, "I've got it!" And it was he who got the patent on it. Still, Edison soon tried to get his version of the system patented. There followed a dispute over who had come up with the idea first. The case ended up in court. Basically, Edison argued that Woods had stolen his design from the Edison and Phelps Company. In the case of *Woods vs. Phelps*, the court twice declared Woods the inventor. At that point, Edison must have figured, "if you can't beat them, join them." He offered Woods a partnership in one of his businesses. Woods, however,

turned him down. He wanted to stay independent. And besides, he had his own company—Woods Electric Company of Cincinnati.

11   The use of Woods's telegraph revolutionized the railroads. It made them much safer and faster. When Woods died in 1910, his inventions had won him worldwide fame. 🍃

If you have been timed while reading this article, enter your reading time below. Then turn to the Words-per-Minute Table on page 71 and look up your reading speed (words per minute). Enter your reading speed on the graph on page 72.

Reading Time: Lesson 1

_____ : _____
Minutes   Seconds

A | Finding the Main Idea

One statement below expresses the main idea of the article. One statement is too general, or too broad. The other statement explains only part of the article; it is too narrow. Label the statements using the following key:

M—Main Idea   **B—Too Broad**   **N—Too Narrow**

_____ 1. Granville Woods overcame racism to become one of the most creative inventors in U.S. history.

_____ 2. Granville Woods tried to satisfy his great curiosity by reading constantly and seeking out private tutors.

_____ 3. Granville Woods was quite possibly the greatest success story of the 19th century.

_____ Score 15 points for a correct M answer.

_____ Score 5 points for each correct B or N answer.

_____ **Total Score:** Finding the Main Idea

B | Recalling Facts

How well do you remember the facts in the article? Put an X in the box next to the answer that correctly completes each statement about the article.

1. Granville Woods left school at the age of
   - ☐ a. 15.
   - ☐ b. 10.
   - ☐ c. 21.

2. Woods's third patent was for
   - ☐ a. a steam boiler furnace.
   - ☐ b. an egg incubator.
   - ☐ c. a machine that combines the telegraph and the telephone.

3. The Multiplex Railway Telegraph allowed
   - ☐ a. passengers to contact the train conductors.
   - ☐ b. conductors to contact other trains and nearby railroad stations.
   - ☐ c. conductors to see other trains more clearly.

4. Woods became involved in a legal fight with
   - ☐ a. Thomas Edison.
   - ☐ b. his own brother.
   - ☐ c. his first employer.

5. Woods's own company was called
   - ☐ a. Woods, Edison, and Phelps Company.
   - ☐ b. Woods Electric Company of Cincinnati.
   - ☐ c. General Electric.

Score 5 points for each correct answer.

_____ **Total Score:** Recalling Facts

C | Making Inferences

When you combine your own experience and information from a text to draw a conclusion that is not directly stated in that text, you are making an inference. Below are five statements that may or may not be inferences based on information in the article. Label the statements using the following key:

C—Correct Inference   **F—Faulty Inference**

_____ 1. Granville Woods couldn't keep a steady job because he didn't work hard enough.

_____ 2. The private teachers that Woods found were willing to teach him without receiving much pay in return.

_____ 3. Racism made Woods an angry and bitter man.

_____ 4. Woods's invention of the Multiplex Railway Telegraph proves that he was better at recognizing and solving problems than Edison was.

_____ 5. Woods's inventions were clever but not very useful.

Score 5 points for each correct answer.

_____ **Total Score:** Making Inferences

D | Using Words Precisely

Each numbered sentence below contains an underlined word or phrase from the article. Following the sentence are three definitions. One definition is closest to the meaning of the underlined word. One definition is opposite or nearly opposite. Label those two definitions using the following key. Do not label the remaining definition.

C—Closest   **O—Opposite or Nearly Opposite**

1. He also <u>sought out</u> private teachers who could help him expand his knowledge of the world.

_____ a. avoided

_____ b. admired

_____ c. tried to find

2. Woods was <u>intrigued</u> by machines and engines of all kinds.

_____ a. disgusted

_____ b. fascinated

_____ c. bored

3. He used his <u>vast</u> knowledge and creativity to solve some of the most perplexing problems of his time.

_____ a. limited

_____ b. valuable

_____ c. extensive

4. He used his vast knowledge and creativity to solve some of the most <u>perplexing</u> problems of his time.

_____ a. puzzling

_____ b. easily understood

_____ c. annoying

5. Woods came up with something that saved untold lives and prevented <u>countless</u> accidents.

_____ a. hardly any

_____ b. unimportant

_____ c. too many to be counted

_____ Score 3 points for each correct C answer.

_____ Score 2 points for each correct O answer.

_____ **Total Score:** Using Words Precisely

Enter the four total scores in the spaces below, and add them together to find your Reading Comprehension Score. Then record your score on the graph on page 73.

Score	Question Type	Lesson 1
_____	Finding the Main Idea	
_____	Recalling Facts	
_____	Making Inferences	
_____	Using Words Precisely	
_____	**Reading Comprehension Score**	

Author's Approach

Put an X in the box next to the correct answer.

1. The main purpose of the first paragraph is to
   ☐ a. inform the reader about Granville Woods's early life.
   ☐ b. describe the qualities of a typical life in the 1860s.
   ☐ c. compare Granville Woods and Thomas Edison.

2. What does the author mean by the statement "As a free African American in the 1860s, he wasn't paid very much"?
   ☐ a. No one was paid much during the 1860s.
   ☐ b. Not many African Americans worked during the 1860s.
   ☐ c. Free African Americans held a low position in American society in the 1860s.

3. From the statements below, choose those that you believe the author would agree with.
   ☐ a. Granville Woods was just as inventive as Thomas Edison.
   ☐ b. Granville Woods had a miserable life.
   ☐ c. Granville Woods was not recognized as a gifted inventor during his lifetime.

_____ Number of correct answers

Record your personal assessment of your work on the Critical Thinking Chart on page 74.

Summarizing and Paraphrasing

Follow the directions provided for questions 1 and 2. Put an X in the box next to the correct answer for question 3.

1. Complete the following one-sentence summary of the article using the lettered phrases from the phrase bank below. Write the letters on the lines.

   Phrase Bank:
   a. some of Woods's inventions
   b. a statement about Woods's reputation at the time of his death
   c. a description of Woods's early life

   The article about Granville Woods begins with _____, goes on to explain _____, and ends with _____.

2. Reread paragraph 11 in the article. Below, write a summary of the paragraph in no more than 25 words.

   _____

   _____

   _____

   _____

   Reread your summary and decide whether it covers the important ideas in the paragraph. Next, decide how to shorten the summary to 15 words or less without leaving out any essential information. Write this summary below.

   _____

   _____

3. Read the statement about the article below. Then read the paraphrase of that statement. Choose the reason that best tells why the paraphrase does not say the same thing as the statement.

   Statement: An article in the *Catholic Tribune* claimed that Granville Woods was "equal, if not superior, to any inventor in the country."

   Paraphrase: According to the *Catholic Tribune*, Granville Woods was an inventor of average ability.

   ☐ a. Paraphrase says too much.

   ☐ b. Paraphrase doesn't say enough.

   ☐ c. Paraphrase doesn't agree with the statement about the article.

   _____ Number of correct answers

   Record your personal assessment of your work on the Critical Thinking Chart on page 74.

Critical Thinking

Follow the directions provided for questions 1 and 3. Put an X in the box next to the correct answer for the other questions.

1. For each statement below, write O if it expresses an opinion or write F if it expresses a fact.

   _____ a. The incubator that Granville Woods invented led to modern incubators.

   _____ b. Granville Woods was a greater inventor than Thomas Edison.

   _____ c. Woods received 45 patents from the U.S. Patent Office.

2. From the article, you can predict that if Edison had offered Woods more money to become a partner in his business, Woods would have

☐ a. still refused Edison's offer.

☐ b. accepted the partnership.

☐ c. asked for even more money.

3. Using what you know about Thomas Edison and what is told about Granville Woods in the article, name three ways Granville Woods is similar to and three ways Granville Woods is different from Thomas Edison. Cite the paragraph number(s) where you found details in the article to support your conclusions.

Similarities

_____

_____

_____

Differences

_____

_____

_____

4. What was the effect of Woods's invention of the Multiplex Railway Telegraph?

☐ a. Woods founded his own electric company.

☐ b. Conductors didn't know what problems were beyond their horizon.

☐ c. Railway travel became faster and safer.

_____ Number of correct answers

Record your personal assessment of your work on the Critical Thinking Chart on page 74.

Personal Response

How do you think Granville Woods felt when Thomas Edison accused him of stealing the design for the Multiplex Railway Telegraph?

_____

_____

_____

_____

Self-Assessment

From reading this article, I have learned

_____

_____

_____

_____

CRITICAL THINKING

MARIE AND PIERRE CURIE
The Discovery of Radium

Marie Curie was the first woman to teach at the Sorbonne in Paris. Here she is shown in her Paris laboratory around 1908.

Suppose you wanted to look at Marie and Pierre Curie's three famous scientific notebooks. You might think that your only problem would be getting to the library in Paris, France, where the notebooks are stored. But you would face another problem as well. Before you could touch the notebooks, you would have to sign a statement. The statement says that you do so *at your own risk*. The notebooks, you see, give off radioactive rays. The rays could kill you.

2   Neither Marie nor Pierre knew the dangers of their work. They didn't know radiation rays could kill people. No one at that time knew it. The Curies spent years working with radium, which gives off the rays. During these years, they never thought about the possible health hazards. In fact, Pierre often carried a sample of radium in his pocket to show his friends. Marie liked to keep some radium by her bed. Its glow, she felt, helped to dispel the darkness. The rays that produced the glow would later cause her death.

3   Marie Curie was born Marya Sklodowska. She left her native Poland for

France in 1891. There Marya changed her first name to the French version, "Marie." There, too, she met Pierre Curie. He was already a fine scientist. She was a brilliant science student. The two fell in love and were married in 1895. This union became one of the great teams in the history of science.

4   In 1897, Marie began work on a doctorate in physics. To get this degree, she had to write a research paper. She chose to focus on the work of Henri Becquerel. A year earlier, Becquerel had discovered an element called uranium. He found that it gave off strange rays. Marie's hunch was that other elements would do the same thing. It was a terrific guess.

5   Marie went to work to prove her theory. At first, she had no luck. She tested metals such as gold and copper. Soon, though, she found that thorium gave off the same rays. Clearly, some elements gave off radiation and others did not.

6   Meanwhile, Pierre, who had been studying crystals, decided to join Marie in her research. Early in 1898, Marie had one more inspired hunch. She decided to test pitchblende. This mineral was well known for its uranium content. Marie and Pierre could not believe the results. Pitchblende gave off much more radiation than

uranium alone. How could that be? Marie and Pierre concluded that there must be something else in the pitchblende. That mysterious something also gave off rays. After more tests on the rays, the Curies found not one new element, but two. They called one *polonium* in honor of Poland. The other they called *radium*.

7   But the Curies' findings so far were mostly just theory. To prove the existence of the new elements, the scientists had to produce them. Marie and Pierre had to isolate enough of these elements to check their atomic weight. To complete that task, they needed tons and tons of costly pitchblende. They didn't have the money to buy it. Luckily, the Austrian government offered help. It gave the Curies all the pitchblende they needed.

8   The next problem was finding a place to work. The principal at a school where Pierre taught came to their aid. He offered them a big old shed. It had an earthen floor and a glass ceiling. Rain often dripped through. The shed was cold and drafty in the winter and hot as a steam bath in the summer. One friend described it as a "cross between a stable and a potato shed."

9   Still, Marie and Pierre spent some of the happiest times of their lives in that

shed. For four years they labored together. It wasn't easy trying to separate the pitchblende. Pitchblende is heavy and hard to work with. "Sometimes," Marie wrote, "I had to spend a whole day stirring a boiling mass with a heavy iron rod nearly as big as myself. I would be broken with fatigue at day's end."

Marie Curie was the first woman to receive a Nobel Prize. In 1903, she and her husband Pierre won the prize for physics. In 1911, Marie was awarded the prize for chemistry.

10   Their hard work paid off. They managed to isolate a fraction of a gram of radium. (The isolation of polonium came later.) It wasn't much, but it was enough. Marie presented her findings for her doctorate in 1903. The teachers who graded her paper said it was the best ever. Friends threw the Curies a party to celebrate. Near the end of the evening, when everyone was seated, Pierre took a tube out of his pocket. It contained some radium. To the wonder of all present, the tube glowed in the dark. One guest, however, couldn't help noticing that Pierre's fingers were badly scarred as if burned. Pierre was finding it hard just to hold the tube.

11   For their breakthrough research, the Curies won the 1903 Nobel Prize in physics. They shared it with Becquerel. Marie was the first woman to win a Nobel Prize. Sadly, this great team did not last much longer. By 1906, Pierre was quite ill. He suffered from radiation poisoning. His condition worsened until he had trouble doing even simple tasks, such as dressing himself. At times, his legs shook so much that he couldn't stand upright. On April 19, 1906, a confused Pierre was walking along a Paris street. He stepped off the curb into oncoming traffic and was struck by a horse-drawn cart. His skull was crushed under one of the wheels.

12   Marie Curie died on July 4, 1934. She was 66 years old. All the years of radiation exposure finally caught up with her. In a way, it was remarkable that she lived as long as she did. No scientist today would spend two minutes working in that lethal shed the way Marie and Pierre Curie did. 🍃

If you have been timed while reading this article, enter your reading time below. Then turn to the Words-per-Minute Table on page 71 and look up your reading speed (words per minute). Enter your reading speed on the graph on page 72.

Reading Time: Lesson 2

_____ : _____
Minutes   Seconds

A | Finding the Main Idea

One statement below expresses the main idea of the article. One statement is too general, or too broad. The other statement explains only part of the article; it is too narrow. Label the statements using the following key:

M—Main Idea   **B—Too Broad**   **N—Too Narrow**

_____ 1. In 1903, Marie and Pierre Curie were awarded the Nobel Prize in physics.

_____ 2. Marie and Pierre Curie dedicated their lives to learning about radium and finally died from their exposure to radiation.

_____ 3. Marie and Pierre Curie were brilliant and courageous scientists.

_____ Score 15 points for a correct M answer.

_____ Score 5 points for each correct B or N answer.

_____ **Total Score:** Finding the Main Idea

B | Recalling Facts

How well do you remember the facts in the article? Put an X in the box next to the answer that correctly completes each statement about the article.

1. When Pierre met Marie, he was a
   - ☐ a. respected scientist.
   - ☐ b. student.
   - ☐ c. school principal.

2. The Curies were surprised that even though pitchblende contained uranium, it
   - ☐ a. was quite heavy.
   - ☐ b. gave off more radiation than uranium alone.
   - ☐ c. was expensive.

3. The two new elements that the Curies found are
   - ☐ a. pitchblende and uranium.
   - ☐ b. uranium and radium.
   - ☐ c. polonium and radium.

4. The Curies did much of their work in
   - ☐ a. a drafty shed.
   - ☐ b. their basement.
   - ☐ c. university laboratories.

5. Eventually, both Curies suffered from
   - ☐ a. malaria.
   - ☐ b. heart disease.
   - ☐ c. radiation poisoning.

Score 5 points for each correct answer.

_____ **Total Score:** Recalling Facts

C | Making Inferences

When you combine your own experience and information from a text to draw a conclusion that is not directly stated in that text, you are making an inference. Below are five statements that may or may not be inferences based on information in the article. Label the statements using the following key:

C—Correct Inference   **F—Faulty Inference**

_____ 1. Scientific research can be dangerous.

_____ 2. Marie Curie regretted spending all those years doing research.

_____ 3. Marie conducted her experiments more carefully than Pierre did.

_____ 4. The Curies were more interested in science than in comfort.

_____ 5. Marie Curie is the only woman in history ever to win a Nobel Prize.

Score 5 points for each correct answer.

_____ **Total Score:** Making Inferences

D | Using Words Precisely

Each numbered sentence below contains an underlined word or phrase from the article. Following the sentence are three definitions. One definition is closest to the meaning of the underlined word. One definition is opposite or nearly opposite. Label those two definitions using the following key. Do not label the remaining definition.

C—Closest   O—Opposite or Nearly Opposite

1. Its glow, she felt, helped to <u>dispel</u> the darkness.

_____ a. celebrate

_____ b. pull together

_____ c. drive away or scatter

2. Early in 1898, Marie had one more <u>inspired</u> hunch.

_____ a. brilliant

_____ b. frightening

_____ c. dull

3. Marie and Pierre had to <u>isolate</u> enough of these elements to check their atomic weight.

_____ a. discover

_____ b. set apart

_____ c. combine

4. "I would be broken with <u>fatigue</u> at day's end."

_____ a. energy and enthusiasm

_____ b. sorrow

_____ c. weariness

5. No scientist today would spend two minutes working in that <u>lethal</u> shed the way the Marie and Pierre Curie did.

_____ a. healthy

_____ b. uncomfortable

_____ c. deadly

_____ Score 3 points for each correct C answer.

_____ Score 2 points for each correct O answer.

_____ **Total Score:** Using Words Precisely

Enter the four total scores in the spaces below, and add them together to find your Reading Comprehension Score. Then record your score on the graph on page 73.

Score	Question Type	Lesson 2
_____	Finding the Main Idea	
_____	Recalling Facts	
_____	Making Inferences	
_____	Using Words Precisely	
_____	**Reading Comprehension Score**	

Author's Approach

Put an X in the box next to the correct answer.

1. What does the author mean by these statements: "Before you could touch the notebooks, you would have to sign a statement. The statement says that you do so *at your own risk*"?

☐ a. The library that houses the notebooks makes unreasonable demands on its users.

☐ b. Those who sign the statement must want to read the notebooks very badly and so they accept the risk.

☐ c. The dangers of touching the notebooks are not worth the risk.

2. What is the author's purpose in writing "Marie and Pierre Curie: The Discovery of Radium"?

☐ a. To encourage the reader to do scientific research

☐ b. To inform the reader about two gifted and dedicated scientists

☐ c. To describe a situation in which people were forced to conduct scientific research against their will

3. From the statements below, choose those that you believe the author would agree with.

☐ a. The Curies found the search for radium exciting.

☐ b. The world would have been a better place if the Curies had not discovered radium.

☐ c. Today's scientists are more careful when they handle radium than the Curies were.

4. What does the author imply by saying "In fact, Pierre often carried a sample of radium in his pocket to show his friends"?

☐ a. Pierre was proud of his scientific breakthrough.

☐ b. Pierre understood the dangers of radiation poisoning.

☐ c. Pierre didn't care about his own health.

_____ Number of correct answers

Record your personal assessment of your work on the Critical Thinking Chart on page 74.

Summarizing and Paraphrasing

Follow the directions provided for question 1. Put an X in the box next to the correct answer for question 2.

1. Look for the important ideas and events in paragraphs 8 and 9. Summarize those paragraphs in one or two sentences.

_____

_____

_____

_____

2. Choose the best one-sentence paraphrase for the following sentence from the article:

"No scientist today would spend two minutes working in that lethal shed the way Marie and Pierre Curie did."

☐ a. No modern scientist would want to work with Marie and Pierre Curie.

☐ b. Today's scientists would avoid the Curies' deadly shed.

☐ c. Modern scientists would need only two minutes to discover what the Curies took years to find in their lethal shed.

_____ Number of correct answers

Record your personal assessment of your work on the Critical Thinking Chart on page 74.

Critical Thinking

Put an X in the box next to the correct answer for questions 1 and 3. Follow the directions provided for the other questions.

1. Which of the following statements from the article is an opinion rather than a fact?

☐ a. "It was a terrific guess."

☐ b. "In 1897, Marie began work on a doctorate in physics."

☐ c. "Pitchblende gave off much more radiation than uranium alone."

CRITICAL THINKING

2. Choose from the letters below to correctly complete the following statement. Write the letters on the lines.

On the positive side, _____, but on the negative side _____.

a.   Marie Curie was born in Poland

b.   the Curies were victims of the radiation they worked with

c.   the Curies expanded human knowledge

3. What was the cause of Pierre's death?

☐ a.   His skull was crushed under the wheels of a cart.

☐ b.   He swallowed poison.

☐ c.   He fell down the stairs.

4. In which paragraph did you find your information or details to answer question 3?

_____

_____ Number of correct answers

Record your personal assessment of your work on the Critical Thinking Chart on page 74.

because

_____

_____

_____

_____

Self-Assessment

I'm proud of how I answered question # _____ in section _____ because

_____

_____

_____

_____

Personal Response

If I were the author, I would add

_____

_____

_____

WHAT'S FOR BREAKFAST?

The first print ad (left) used by W. K. Kellogg to advertise his cornflakes appeared in 1906.

What did you have for breakfast this morning? If you had been born in the United States, say, 150 years ago, chances are good that you would have had an English-style breakfast. That would have meant some pork, maybe a leftover sausage or two, greasy fried potatoes, and tons of buttered bread. All in all, it would have been a pretty unhealthy way to start your day. Not surprisingly, many people at the time suffered from upset stomach, gout, and other gastric disorders.

2   Health reformers wanted something done. They wanted to shape up people's diets. Meat was one food on their hit list. It was unhealthy and, they said, could drive people mad. White bread, they claimed, was overly refined. Hearty whole grains were better. And they considered coffee and tea to be nothing but poisons.

3   There was a problem, however. This "bad" food tasted good. So how could the reformers get folks to eat right? Could they develop breakfast foods that were healthy *and* tasted good, too?

4   Many reformers deserve an "A" for effort. Sylvester Graham, for example, urged people to put bran back in their

breads. His own concoction is still with us—the graham cracker. Another successful reformer was a German immigrant named Ferdinand Schumacher. In the early 1800s, he noticed that Americans fed oats to their horses. He wondered why people didn't eat the healthy grain themselves. He decided that one reason was that oatmeal took hours to boil. Schumacher came up with a kind of oatmeal that didn't take that long. Soon he was known as the "Oatmeal King of America."

5   Henry Perky invented the first cold breakfast cereal. He began by heating wheat berries until they were softened. By drawing these berries through rollers, he turned them into threads. From these, Perky made airy biscuits called "shredded wheat."

6   The real kings of the breakfast food revolution, though, were Doctor John Harvey Kellogg and his younger brother Will Keith Kellogg. John and Will lived in Battle Creek, Michigan, and belonged to a religious group known as Seventh Day Adventists. Around 1878, John became director of an Adventist-run hospital and health spa. He hired his brother to be his assistant. They changed the name of the hospital and spa to the Battle Creek Sanitarium. To most people, the institution was known as the "San." Many

famous people went there to "take the cure." Patients included John D. Rockefeller, Thomas Edison, and Henry Ford. The "cure" consisted of lots of exercise and a strict low-fat diet. Patients could not eat meat of any kind. They couldn't drink coffee, tea, or alcohol. And, of course, they couldn't smoke.

7   Often, the spa food was served with yummy peanut butter. Even so, some patients complained that the food tasted like straw. The San's meals drove some patients away. Others slipped off to the nearby Red Onion Cafe for a quick, juicy steak.

8   John, the idealist, ran the San while Will, the realist, was the business manager. Both knew that their future depended on their ability to improve the tasteless food. So they began to experiment. They blended whole grains, fruits, and fresh vegetables. In their laboratory, they baked, boiled, steamed, and pressed the mixtures, trying to find the right taste and texture. Soon they came up with a decent substitute for coffee.

They made a new kind of milk out of soy beans. They developed imitation pork, meat, veal, and chicken made from nuts and wheat gluten.

9   John and Will also worked to make a low-starch, easy-to-chew, whole wheat breakfast food. Doctor John had a practi-

John H. Kellogg at 86 years old in 1938

cal reason. "I prescribed [a hard biscuit] for an old lady, and she broke her false teeth on it. She demanded that I pay her $10 for her false teeth," John said. "I began to think that we ought to have a ready-cooked food which would not break people's teeth. I puzzled over that a good deal."

10   John wanted something like shredded wheat, only softer and better. Perhaps small pieces of toasted bread, he thought, would do the trick. So he and Will boiled batch after batch of whole wheat and pressed it. Mostly, however, they got nothing but a messy paste. They tried rolling the gooey dough through pins like those on an old laundry wringer. It wasn't a pretty sight. The blobs of wheat just stuck to the rollers.

11   Then one day in 1894, they got lucky. John told Will to boil up yet another mixture of wheat. John took the batch to the lab where he had his rollers set up. Before they could press the mixture, the two men were called away. The wheat mixture was left sitting in a hopper. Because John refused to use sugar or salt, the wheat quickly went rancid. When the two men returned, they decided to roll the wheat anyway. To their astonishment, the moldy wheat broke up into thin flakes. John and Will baked and dried the flakes, which turned out crispy—if a bit stale.

12   What the brothers had discovered was not a new kind of bread, but the secret for making a new ready-to-eat breakfast cereal. They called it "tempering" the wheat. "Tempering" meant letting it stand for several hours. Before long, they perfected the procedure so the mixture did not become moldy. They applied the same technique to rice and corn as well as wheat. Now the patients at the San could choose between delicious wheat flakes, rice flakes, and corn flakes. Some even asked to have the cereals sent to their homes after they left the San.

13   John did not see the huge potential of his accidental discovery. His sole interest was his patients. Will was different. He wanted to sell the flakes to the public. John wanted the flakes ground up and blended with soy bean milk. Will insisted that they leave the flakes alone. The flakes, he declared, should be packaged whole just as they came out of the oven. Years later, Will left the San and started his own cereal company. He called it the "Battle Creek Toasted Corn Flake Company." His company became a great success. Its most famous product was Kellogg's Corn Flakes.

14   Will Kellogg wasn't the only one to make a fortune on breakfast cereal. Another early giant in the field was Charles W. Post. He was a former patient at the San. He heard about Kellogg's new cereal flakes. In 1896, he came up with his own cereal, which he called Grape-Nuts. First he tried to sell it as a grain beverage. That effort failed. Then he got the bright idea to market Grape-Nuts as a breakfast food. Grape-Nuts was a huge hit even though the cereal had neither grapes nor nuts in it. The name came from Post's imagination. He thought that the baking process created "grape sugar" and that the final product had a nutty crunch.

15   Thanks largely to Post and the Kellogg brothers, people don't have to eat pork and potatoes for breakfast anymore. An average supermarket offers about 70 varieties of ready-to-eat cereals. They come in all sorts of dazzling shapes and eye-popping colors. But would they please the old-time reformers? It is hard to imagine old Doctor John Harvey Kellogg eating a bowl of today's modern cereal laced with sugar and chemicals. Plain old corn flakes would be much more to his liking. 🌿

If you have been timed while reading this article, enter your reading time below. Then turn to the Words-per-Minute Table on page 71 and look up your reading speed (words per minute). Enter your reading speed on the graph on page 72.

Reading Time: **Lesson 3**

_____ : _____
Minutes   Seconds

A Finding the Main Idea

One statement below expresses the main idea of the article. One statement is too general, or too broad. The other statement explains only part of the article; it is too narrow. Label the statements using the following key:

M—Main Idea   **B—Too Broad**   **N—Too Narrow**

_____ 1. Health reformers during the 19th century were determined to improve the American diet; we eat some of their inventions, such as corn flakes, every morning

_____ 2. Corn flakes were invented at a health spa in Battle Creek, Michigan.

_____ 3. The American diet has changed over the past two centuries.

_____ Score 15 points for a correct M answer.

_____ Score 5 points for each correct B or N answer.

_____ **Total Score:** Finding the Main Idea

B Recalling Facts

How well do you remember the facts in the article? Put an X in the box next to the answer that correctly completes each statement about the article.   .

1. Some health reformers believed that coffee and tea were
   ☐ a. poisons.
   ☐ b. too expensive.
   ☐ c. filled with too much fat.

2. Sylvester Graham's goal was to
   ☐ a. make a ready-to-eat cereal.
   ☐ b. encourage people to eat more oatmeal.
   ☐ c. add bran to the American diet.

3. "Tempering" the wheat means
   ☐ a. growing mold in it.
   ☐ b. letting it stand for several hours.
   ☐ c. heating it up and then cooling it down quickly.

4. The Kelloggs ran a
   ☐ a. health spa.
   ☐ b. restaurant.
   ☐ c. grocery store.

5. Grape-Nuts were invented by
   ☐ a. Will Kellogg.
   ☐ b. Charles W. Post.
   ☐ c. Ferdinand Schumacher.

Score 5 points for each correct answer.

_____ **Total Score:** Recalling Facts

C Making Inferences

When you combine your own experience and information from a text to draw a conclusion that is not directly stated in that text, you are making an inference. Below are five statements that may or may not be inferences based on information in the article. Label the statements using the following key:

C—Correct Inference   **F—Faulty Inference**

_____ 1. During the 19th century, no one suspected that smoking was harmful to your health.

_____ 2. Peanut butter can cover up the taste of any food.

_____ 3. People in the 19th century were more concerned about their diets than people are today.

_____ 4. In the morning, people like the speed and convenience of cold cereals.

_____ 5. Sometimes, important discoveries happen by accident.

Score 5 points for each correct answer.

_____ **Total Score:** Making Inferences

D Using Words Precisely

Each numbered sentence below contains an underlined word or phrase from the article. Following the sentence are three definitions. One definition is closest to the meaning of the underlined word. One definition is opposite or nearly opposite. Label those two definitions using the following key. Do not label the remaining definition.

C—Closest   **O—Opposite or Nearly Opposite**

1. Hearty whole grains were better.

_____ a. full of empty calories

_____ b. cold

_____ c. nourishing

2. His own concoction is still with us—the graham cracker.

_____ a. mixture

_____ b. single element

_____ c. invention

3. They developed imitation pork, meat, veal, and chicken made from nuts and wheat gluten.

_____ a. authentic

_____ b. delicious

_____ c. substitute

4. Because John refused to use sugar or salt, the wheat quickly went rancid.

_____ a. black

_____ b. fresh

_____ c. rotten

5. It is hard to imagine old Doctor John Harvey Kellogg eating a bowl of today's modern cereal <u>laced with</u> sugar and chemicals.

_____ a. free from

_____ b. mixed with

_____ c. protected by

_____ Score 3 points for each correct C answer.

_____ Score 2 points for each correct O answer.

_____ **Total Score:** Using Words Precisely

Enter the four total scores in the spaces below, and add them together to find your Reading Comprehension Score. Then record your score on the graph on page 73.

Score	Question Type	Lesson 3
_____	Finding the Main Idea	
_____	Recalling Facts	
_____	Making Inferences	
_____	Using Words Precisely	
_____	**Reading Comprehension Score**	

Author's Approach

Put an X in the box next to the correct answer.

1. The author uses the first sentence of the article to
   - ☐ a. introduce the reader to the general topic of the article.
   - ☐ b. describe the qualities of cold cereal.
   - ☐ c. compare a traditional English-style breakfast and cold cereal.

2. What does the author mean by the statement "Soon he [Schumacher] was known as the "Oatmeal King of America"?
   - ☐ a. Oatmeal became so popular that Schumacher was made king of America.
   - ☐ b. Schumacher was proud of his invention and saw himself as the king of America.
   - ☐ c. Schumacher was admired all over America for his popular invention.

3. The main purpose of the first paragraph is to
   - ☐ a. create a solemn mood.
   - ☐ b. describe the English-style breakfast and express an opinion about its healthfulness.
   - ☐ c. suggest a good alternative to the traditional breakfast.

4. Choose the statement below that best describes the author's position in paragraph 15.
   - ☐ a. All ready-to-eat cereals are much healthier than pork and potatoes.
   - ☐ b. Though we have more breakfast choices than before, they may not all be healthy.
   - ☐ c. Doctor John Kellogg would be proud of the trend he started.

_____ Number of correct answers

Record your personal assessment of your work on the Critical Thinking Chart on page 74.

CRITICAL THINKING

Summarizing and Paraphrasing

Follow the directions provided for question 1. Put an X in the box next to the correct answer for the other questions.

1. Complete the following one-sentence summary of the article using the lettered phrases from the phrase bank below. Write the letters on the lines.

    > **Phrase Bank:**
    > a. how various reformers invented new breakfast foods
    > b. a criticism of some of today's cereals
    > c. a description of an English-style breakfast

    The article about the invention of breakfast foods begins with
    _____, goes on to explain _____, and ends with _____.

2. Read the statement about the article below. Then read the paraphrase of that statement. Choose the reason that best tells why the paraphrase does not say the same thing as the statement.

    Statement: Many famous patients stayed at the Battle Creek Sanitarium.

    Paraphrase: Famous people such as John D. Rockefeller, Thomas Edison, and Henry Ford stayed at the Battle Creek Sanitarium which the Kellogg brothers ran.

    ☐ a. Paraphrase says too much.

    ☐ b. Paraphrase doesn't say enough.

    ☐ c. Paraphrase doesn't agree with the statement about the article.

3. Choose the sentence that correctly restates the following sentence from the article:

    "What the brothers had discovered was not a new kind of bread, but the secret for making a new ready-to-eat breakfast cereal."

    ☐ a. The brothers had discovered both a new kind of bread and a new breakfast cereal.

    ☐ b. The brothers didn't care about discovering a new breakfast cereal; they were interested in making bread.

    ☐ c. Instead of making a new bread, the brothers had invented a way to make a ready-to-eat cereal.

    > _____ Number of correct answers
    >
    > Record your personal assessment of your work on the Critical Thinking Chart on page 74.

Critical Thinking

Put an X in the box next to the correct answer for questions 1 and 2. Follow the directions provided for the other questions.

1. Which of the following statements from the article is an opinion rather than a fact?

    ☐ a. "Henry Perky invented the first cold breakfast cereal."

    ☐ b. "Before they could press the mixture, the two men were called away."

    ☐ c. "Many reformers deserve an "A" for effort."

2. Using information in paragraph 15, you can predict that

☐ a. Doctor Kellogg will return to have a bowl of cereal.

☐ b. modern reformers will recommend that sugar and chemicals be removed from cold cereal.

☐ c. supermarkets will soon stop selling cold cereals.

3. Using what is told about John Kellogg and Will Kellogg in the article, name three ways John Kellogg is similar to and three ways he is different from Will Kellogg. Cite the paragraph number(s) where you found details in the article to support your conclusions.

Similarities

_____

_____

_____

Differences

_____

_____

_____

4. Read paragraph 7. Then choose from the letters below to correctly complete the following statement. Write the letters on the lines.

According to paragraph 7, _____ because _____.

a. many famous patients went to the Battle Creek Sanitarium

b. patients went to a nearby café for tasty food

c. the food served at the Battle Creek Sanitarium tasted like straw

_____ Number of correct answers

Record your personal assessment of your work on the Critical Thinking Chart on page 74.

Personal Response

What was most surprising or interesting to you about this article?

_____

_____

_____

_____

Self-Assessment

When reading the article, I was having trouble with

_____

_____

_____

_____

CRITICAL THINKING

BALBOA AND THE PACIFIC

Balboa may have found scenery like that pictured at the left when he reached the Pacific coast of Panama.

Vasco de Balboa had his ups and downs. As a daring young Spaniard, Balboa sailed to America in 1500 in search of gold and glory. He found neither. Instead, he ended up working as a pig farmer on the island we now call Haiti. Worse, Balboa was an awful farmer. He borrowed money that he could not pay back. Soon he had a storm of angry creditors after him.

2 In 1510, Balboa fled his debts. He became a stowaway. He slipped onto a ship headed for a new Spanish colony called Panama. Once aboard, he sealed himself inside a large food cask. After the ship was far out to sea, he emerged from the barrel. Captain Martin de Enciso was so furious he nearly tossed Balboa over the side. But he soon thought better of it. Balboa might come in handy in the new colony. He was a seasoned fighter. And he was familiar with Panama. Over the past 10 years he had visited the region a couple of times.

3 When the ship landed, Balboa joined the Spanish army. But under Enciso's inept rule, the colony on the Gulf of

Darien floundered. Enciso could not cope with the hostile Indians. He did not know what to do about the dwindling food supplies. Soon the settlers voted to oust Enciso. They shipped him back to Spain. In his place, they installed Balboa. Balboa moved the colony across the gulf to a spot where the Indians were less hostile. This saved the colony from destruction.

4   Unlike other conquistadors, Balboa got along with the Indians most of the time. He made friends with the Careta Indians after subduing them by force. As a favor to them, Balboa defeated their arch enemies— the Ponca tribe. The Careta rewarded Balboa by telling him about the Comogra. This was a wealthy tribe to the north. Balboa took his men to visit the tribe. The gold they saw there stunned them. This was indeed the golden paradise of their dreams.

5   The Comogra, seeing the greed in the Spaniards' eyes, offered up some gold baubles. But Balboa's men began to quarrel over these items. They argued about who would get which one. The Comogra leader was disgusted by the Spaniards' thoughtless greed. He wanted to get rid of the intruders as quickly as possible. And so he told them of a land on a great ocean, the legendary Other Sea, across the hills of Panama. There, he said,

the rivers ran with gold and the beaches were laced with pearls.

6   Balboa did not need to hear more. The story set his mind on fire. All at once it seemed as though gold and glory were within his grasp. He wanted to be the first European to lay eyes on this mysterious sea. That feat would surely impress Ferdinand, the Spanish king. And Balboa did need to please the king. After all, Balboa was just the *temporary* governor of the colony. At any time, the king could name someone new to the post. Balboa's enemies back in Spain were probably urging the king to do just that.

7   Balboa knew the trip to the Other Sea would require careful planning. Hostile tribes lived in the hills. Also, Balboa's men would have to hack their way through the dense jungle and cross murky swamps. At the same time, they would have to cope with fierce heat, deadly animals, and strange diseases.

8   It took two years to prepare for the journey. At last, on September 6, 1513, the march inland began. Balboa had with him 190 soldiers. He had hundreds of Indians who served as porters and guides. He also took a pack of ferocious bloodhounds just in case of trouble.

9   The route Balboa took across Panama covered just 45 miles. But a more arduous

45 miles would be hard to imagine. The jungle was so thick with trees it blotted out the sun. Sometimes the men were lucky to walk just one mile in a whole day. And there were plenty of nasty things

This 19th-century lithograph depicts Balboa claiming the South Sea (Pacific Ocean) for Spain on September 27, 1513.

along the way. These included vampire bats, pit vipers, and poison arrow frogs. There was a tree whose sap could cause blindness. And there were other dangers, including fire ants, spiders, and coral snakes. Dozens of deadly diseases awaited the unlucky. One disease caused a man's internal organs to explode. Another left victims with internal worms that could eat a man from the inside out.

10   On top of all this, the local Indians didn't like strangers entering their lands. Over 600 Quarecan warriors attacked the Spanish. Since the warriors had only flimsy shields and bows and arrows, however, the match was uneven. The Spanish had armor, guns, and swords. In addition, they had those fearsome war dogs. At one point, Balboa let the bloodhounds loose in an Indian village. The dogs killed everyone in sight.

11   On September 25, Balboa approached "a bare high hill." One of his guides told him the great sea could be seen from the top of the hill. Balboa signaled a halt. He wanted to climb the hill alone. At the summit, Balboa saw a vast stretch of blue water.

12   One of his men wrote what happened next. "[Balboa] turned toward the troops, very happy, lifting eyes and hands to heaven…and then he knelt down on both knees and gave much thanks to God for…allowing him to discover that sea."

13   Two days later, the men reached the water. Balboa named it the "South Sea." (It was Ferdinand Magellan who first called it the Pacific Ocean.) Balboa plunged into the waves holding a sword and the Spanish flag. He proclaimed "these seas and lands" to be the "royal possession" of Spain.

14   Although he found no gold or pearls on his journey, discovering the Pacific Ocean was probably the high point in Balboa's life. But it was mostly downhill from there. While he was marching across Panama, his worst fear came true. Ferdinand named a permanent governor to the colony. The man's name was Pedro Arias Davila, or just Pedrarias. He and Balboa became bitter rivals. Officials in Spain tried to patch things up, but they failed. Pedrarias had Balboa arrested on false charges of being a traitor to the Crown. Balboa was quickly tried and found guilty. He was sentenced to death. On January 15, 1519, Vasco de Balboa, the great discoverer of the Pacific, was beheaded.

If you have been timed while reading this article, enter your reading time below. Then turn to the Words-per-Minute Table on page 71 and look up your reading speed (words per minute). Enter your reading speed on the graph on page 72.

Reading Time: Lesson 3

_____ : _____
Minutes   Seconds

A | **Finding the Main Idea**

One statement below expresses the main idea of the article. One statement is too general, or too broad. The other statement explains only part of the article; it is too narrow. Label the statements using the following key:

M—Main Idea   B—Too Broad   N—Too Narrow

_____ 1. For a while, Balboa worked as a pig farmer on the island of Haiti.

_____ 2. The life of an adventurer is not always pleasant.

_____ 3. Balboa was a Spanish adventurer whose main claim to fame was that he was the first European to see the Pacific Ocean.

_____ Score 15 points for a correct M answer.

_____ Score 5 points for each correct B or N answer.

_____ **Total Score:** Finding the Main Idea

B | **Recalling Facts**

How well do you remember the facts in the article? Put an X in the box next to the answer that correctly completes each statement about the article.

1. On the ship that brought him to Panama, Balboa hid in
   ☐ a. the captain's room.
   ☐ b. a food barrel.
   ☐ c. a lifeboat.

2. The tribe that had a great deal of gold was
   ☐ a. the Comogra tribe.
   ☐ b. the Careta tribe.
   ☐ c. the Ponca tribe.

3. Balboa needed to impress the king so that he could be named
   ☐ a. permanent governor of Panama.
   ☐ b. king of America.
   ☐ c. governor of Haiti.

4. The distance Balboa walked across Panama to the Pacific was
   ☐ a. 10 miles.
   ☐ b. 25 miles.
   ☐ c. 45 miles.

5. Balboa was tried and found guilty of
   ☐ a. theft in office.
   ☐ b. treason.
   ☐ c. killing innocent Indians.

Score 5 points for each correct answer.

_____ **Total Score:** Recalling Facts

C | Making Inferences

When you combine your own experience and information from a text to draw a conclusion that is not directly stated in that text, you are making an inference. Below are five statements that may or may not be inferences based on information in the article. Label the statements using the following key:

C—Correct Inference   F—Faulty Inference

_____ 1. Balboa had great respect for the native people already living in America.

_____ 2. No one had ever seen the Pacific Ocean before Balboa arrived.

_____ 3. Haiti was colonized earlier than Panama was.

_____ 4. Gold was easy to find in Panama.

_____ 5. Balboa was driven by ambition and greed.

Score 5 points for each correct answer.

_____ **Total Score:** Making Inferences

D | Using Words Precisely

Each numbered sentence below contains an underlined word or phrase from the article. Following the sentence are three definitions. One definition is closest to the meaning of the underlined word. One definition is opposite or nearly opposite. Label those two definitions using the following key. Do not label the remaining definition.

C—Closest   O—Opposite or Nearly Opposite

1. He was a <u>seasoned</u> fighter.

_____ a. summer

_____ b. new

_____ c. experienced

2. But under Enciso's <u>inept</u> rule, the colony on the Gulf of Darien floundered

_____ a. skillful

_____ b. clumsy

_____ c. unjust

3. He did not know what to do about the <u>dwindling</u> food supplies.

_____ a. rotten

_____ b. shrinking

_____ c. expanding

4. Soon the settlers voted to <u>oust</u> Enciso.

_____ a. hire

_____ b. report on

_____ c. get rid of

5. He made friends with the Careta Indians after <u>subduing</u> them by force.

_____ a. bringing under control

_____ b. following

_____ c. giving greater powers and privileges

_____ Score 3 points for each correct C answer.

_____ Score 2 points for each correct O answer.

_____ **Total Score:** Using Words Precisely

Enter the four total scores in the spaces below, and add them together to find your Reading Comprehension Score. Then record your score on the graph on page 73.

Score	Question Type	Lesson 4
_____	Finding the Main Idea	
_____	Recalling Facts	
_____	Making Inferences	
_____	Using Words Precisely	
_____	**Reading Comprehension Score**	

Author's Approach

Put an X in the box next to the correct answer.

1. The author uses the first sentence of the article to
☐ a. inform the reader about the many changes in Balboa's life.
☐ b. describe the personal qualities of Balboa.
☐ c. compare Balboa and other European explorers.

2. From the statements below, choose those that you believe the author would agree with.
☐ a. Balboa was a hero that everyone admires.
☐ b. Balboa was not fit to become governor of Panama since he didn't have any experience in running large projects.
☐ c. It was unfair that Balboa was found guilty of being a traitor.

3. Judging by statements from the article "Balboa and the Pacific," you can conclude that the author wants the reader to think that
☐ a. Balboa was executed unjustly.
☐ b. Balboa soon would have developed excellent farming skills if he had continued to work on a pig farm in Haiti.
☐ c. Martin de Enciso was an excellent problem solver.

4. The author tells this story mainly by
☐ a. retelling his or her personal experiences.
☐ b. relating events in the order they happened.
☐ c. using his or her imagination and creativity.

_____ Number of correct answers

Record your personal assessment of your work on the Critical Thinking Chart on page 74.

CRITICAL THINKING

Summarizing and Paraphrasing

Put an X in the box next to the correct answer for question 1. Follow the directions provided for question 2.

1. Below are summaries of the article. Choose the summary that says all the most important things about the article but in the fewest words.

☐ a. Balboa was not always successful. In fact, he was an unsuccessful farmer in Haiti and unsuccessfully tried to be named governor of Panama. One of the few things he did accomplish was to see the Pacific Ocean before any other European, but after that he started a rivalry between himself and the permanent governor. Finally, he was tried and convicted of treason and was beheaded.

☐ b. Although Balboa first came to Panama as a stowaway, he soon was put in charge of the struggling colony. He worked hard, trying to become its permanent governor.

☐ c. Balboa was a competent leader who became the first European to see the Pacific Ocean. Eventually he was found guilty of treason and was beheaded.

2. Reread paragraph 2 in the article. Below, write a summary of the paragraph in no more than 25 words.

_____

_____

_____

_____

Reread your summary and decide whether it covers the important ideas in the paragraph. Next, decide how to shorten the summary to 15 words or less without leaving out any essential information. Write this summary below.

_____

_____

_____

_____ Number of correct answers

Record your personal assessment of your work on the Critical Thinking Chart on page 74.

Critical Thinking

Follow the directions provided for questions 1 and 2. Put an X in the box next to the correct answer for the other questions.

1. Choose from the letters below to correctly complete the following statement. Write the letters on the lines.

   In the article, _____ and _____ were different in their ability to run a colony.

   a. Vasco de Balboa

   b. Martin de Enciso

   c. Ferdinand Magellan

2. Read paragraph 14. Then choose from the letters below to correctly complete the following statement. Write the letters on the lines.

According to paragraph 14, _____ because _____.

   a. Ferdinand chose a permanent governor while Balboa was marching across Panama

   b. Balboa was tried for treason and beheaded

   c. Balboa and the governor, Pedrarias, were bitter rivals

3. Of the following theme categories, which would this story fit into?

   ☐ a. Keep trying and you will eventually succeed.

   ☐ b. It pays to be in the right place at the right time.

   ☐ c. Virtue is its own reward.

4. What did you have to do to answer question 1?

   ☐ a. find an opinion (what someone thinks about something)

   ☐ b. find a contrast (how things are different)

   ☐ c. draw a conclusion (a sensible statement based on the text and your experience)

_____ Number of correct answers

Record your personal assessment of your work on the Critical Thinking Chart on page 74.

Personal Response

How do you think Balboa felt when he found out that someone else had been named permanent governor of Panama?

_____

_____

_____

_____

Self-Assessment

One good question about this article that was not asked would be

_____

_____

_____

_____

and the answer is

_____

_____

_____

_____

CRITICAL THINKING

"COLONEL DRAKE'S FOLLY"

in al Drake In 1860

Colonel Drake (right) in front of his "folly," the first oil well in Titusville, Pennsylvania

For Edwin Drake it was a matter of being in the right place at the right time. In the summer of 1857, the 38-year-old Drake was staying at the Tontine Hotel in New Haven, Connecticut. He was sick and out of work. Still, Drake struck up a conversation with James Townsend, another guest at the hotel. Townsend, one of the chief owners of the Seneca Oil Company, was fascinated by oil. So, too, was Drake.

2   Oil itself was no mystery. Since the dawn of history, people had used it for medicine. Native Americans has also used it to make paint. By the mid-1800s, Americans had found new uses for oil. They discovered that it made a terrific axle grease. They also learned that it could be burned in lamps. No, the mystery of oil wasn't what to do with it, but how to get enough of it. In some places, it just seeped up through the earth. But the oil gathered from such seepage wasn't nearly enough. A few barrels of oil wasn't going to change the world. But if a way could be found to get larger amounts of oil, there would be no limit to its power.

3   That thought inspired Townsend and Drake. Townsend asked the former store

clerk to go to Pennsylvania to check out Titusville, a small country town. There, oil seeped through the ground. Some oil was even getting into local wells and rivers. Surely, Townsend thought, some way could be found to get at and collect this oil. Drake, suddenly feeling better, agreed to go. He arrived in Titusville in December. To impress the local residents, Townsend sent him letters addressed to "Colonel" Edwin Drake. The bogus title stuck.

4   Drake liked what he saw in Titusville. He wrote an optimistic report back to Townsend. After reading Drake's report, the Seneca Oil Company leased a tract of land in Titusville. As a reward, the company put Drake in charge of finding a way to get at the oil.

5   At first, Drake thought he could *mine* the oil like coal. In other words, he tried to dig a big hole in the ground. But all such efforts failed. The ground often caved in, or else the hole filled up with water from underground springs. Most of the time, Drake managed to produce just three or four gallons of oil a day. On a very good day, he might produce six gallons. Later, Drake improved his methods and gathered 10 gallons a day. Still, this wasn't nearly enough. Drake hired men to build a shaft into the earth the way miners do. That didn't work

either. The shaft quickly flooded with water.

6   Then Drake had a new idea. Instead of digging, he thought, why not bore for oil? People already knew how to drill for water. Why not try it for oil? Drake hired local driller William "Uncle Billy" Smith and his two sons to give it a try. When the local people heard about Drake's plan, they laughed heartily. They dubbed his project "Colonel Drake's Folly."

7   Meanwhile, Drake was battling financial problems. The money the company had given him was long gone. Gone, too, was the money he had invested himself. But he refused to quit. To keep his hopes alive, he had to borrow money from friends.

8   The project continued. To make the drilling easier, the men used a steam engine and cast iron pipes. This new tactic simply made the residents howl louder. Drake, of course, had no idea how far down the drillers would have to go in order to find oil. Nobody had ever attempted it before. Smith and his sons eventually hit bedrock, which was mostly shale, after passing the 30-foot level. Using the steam engine, they were able to drill through the shale. The pace was slow, however—only three feet a day. Even at that speed, there were problems.

Sometimes the shale caved in. Once, the steam engine itself caught fire. The residents of Titusville thought that was terribly funny.

9   By August 27, 1859, even Drake began to despair. He had already spent 19 months in Titusville. He hadn't struck oil,

COLONEL E. L. DRAKE.

Edwin L. Drake, the founder of the American petroleum industry

and the money he had borrowed was nearly gone. Late that afternoon, Smith's drill slipped into a crevice after reaching 69½ feet. Smith left the drill in place and called it a day. The next morning he returned to check on the well. When Smith looked down into the pipe, he saw oil! It was oozing from the bottom of the well. He sent one of his sons running into town to give Drake the happy news.

10   The word of Drake's discovery touched off an oil boom as wild as any gold rush. Speculators roamed western Pennsylvania trying to persuade farmers to sell or lease their land. Hundreds of oil companies began to drill for "black gold." Boom towns, such as the infamous Pithole, sprang up almost overnight. Where trees once stood, a vast forest of oil derricks took their place. By 1860, Pennsylvania wells were pumping out half a million barrels of oil a year. Two years later, the production of refined oil had jumped to 3 million barrels. And by 1870, it reached more than 140 million barrels! In a few short years, oil had become the world's main source of light, heat, and energy. Many people in the oil business made money hand over fist.

11   And what about Colonel Drake? Sadly, his luck ran out on August 27, the day his diggers struck oil. Drake neglected to patent his method of drilling for oil. Without a patent, others could copy his method without paying him a dime. Ten years later, Drake was again ailing and nearly broke. News of his misery spread. Pennsylvania voted to give him a yearly pension of $1,500.

12   Colonel Edwin Drake died in 1884. Seventeen years later, Standard Oil Company put up a monument in his honor. It was built in Titusville. The inscription calls him the "Founder of the Petroleum Industry."

If you have been timed while reading this article, enter your reading time below. Then turn to the Words-per-Minute Table on page 71 and look up your reading speed (words per minute). Enter your reading speed on the graph on page 72.

Reading Time: Lesson 5

_____ : _____
Minutes   Seconds

A | Finding the Main Idea

One statement below expresses the main idea of the article. One statement is too general, or too broad. The other statement explains only part of the article; it is too narrow. Label the statements using the following key:

M—Main Idea   B—Too Broad   N—Too Narrow

_____ 1. In spite of ridicule and financial problems, Edwin Drake supervised the drilling of the first successful oil well.

_____ 2. Edwin Drake hired William Smith and his sons to drill for oil in Titusville, Pennsylvania.

_____ 3. Oil is an important fuel, used all over the world.

_____ Score 15 points for a correct M answer.

_____ Score 5 points for each correct B or N answer.

_____ **Total Score:** Finding the Main Idea

B | Recalling Facts

How well do you remember the facts in the article? Put an X in the box next to the answer that correctly completes each statement about the article.

1. James Townsend was
   - ☐ a. owner of Seneca Oil Company.
   - ☐ b. owner of the Tontine Hotel in Connecticut.
   - ☐ c. owner of Standard Oil Company.

2. When Townsend sent letters to Drake in Titusville, he addressed them
   - ☐ a. "Uncle Billy."
   - ☐ b. "Colonel" Edwin Drake.
   - ☐ c. "Founder of the Petroleum Industry."

3. Drake found that the most successful method of getting oil was to
   - ☐ a. dig a big hole and mine the oil like coal.
   - ☐ b. build a shaft like coal miners do.
   - ☐ c. drill for it, just as people drill for water.

4. Smith found oil after drilling down
   - ☐ a. 30 feet.
   - ☐ b. 55½ feet.
   - ☐ c. 69½ feet.

5. Drake didn't get rich with his method of drilling for oil because
   - ☐ a. he hadn't patented his idea.
   - ☐ b. he wasn't skillful in handling money.
   - ☐ c. the oil companies cheated him.

Score 5 points for each correct answer.

_____ **Total Score:** Recalling Facts

C Making Inferences

When you combine your own experience and information from a text to draw a conclusion that is not directly stated in that text, you are making an inference. Below are five statements that may or may not be inferences based on information in the article. Label the statements using the following key:

C—Correct Inference   F—Faulty Inference

_____ 1. Everyone in Pennsylvania became rich after Drake found a way to get at the oil there.

_____ 2. Pennsylvania is the only place in the world where oil can be found.

_____ 3. Doing new things in new ways often takes courage.

_____ 4. Most of the residents of Titusville believed in and supported Drake.

_____ 5. The state of Pennsylvania felt that it owed Drake something after what he had given the state.

Score 5 points for each correct answer.

_____ **Total Score:** Making Inferences

D Using Words Precisely

Each numbered sentence below contains an underlined word or phrase from the article. Following the sentence are three definitions. One definition is closest to the meaning of the underlined word. One definition is opposite or nearly opposite. Label those two definitions using the following key. Do not label the remaining definition.

C—Closest   O—Opposite or Nearly Opposite

1. The bogus title stuck.

_____ a. fake

_____ b. silly

_____ c. genuine

2. He wrote an optimistic report back to Townsend.

_____ a. gloomy

_____ b. cheerful

_____ c. factual

3. By August 27, 1859, even Drake began to despair.

_____ a. forget

_____ b. become hopeful

_____ c. lose hope

4. It [oil] was oozing from the bottom of the well.

_____ a. giving off a bad odor

_____ b. seeping

_____ c. exploding

5. Boom towns, such as the <u>infamous</u> Pithole, sprang up almost overnight.

_____ a. respected

_____ b. popular

_____ c. shameful or disgraceful

_____ Score 3 points for each correct C answer.

_____ Score 2 points for each correct O answer.

_____ **Total Score:** Using Words Precisely

Enter the four total scores in the spaces below, and add them together to find your Reading Comprehension Score. Then record your score on the graph on page 73.

Score	Question Type	Lesson 5
_____	Finding the Main Idea	
_____	Recalling Facts	
_____	Making Inferences	
_____	Using Words Precisely	
_____	**Reading Comprehension Score**	

Author's Approach

Put an X in the box next to the correct answer.

1. The main purpose of the first paragraph is to

☐ a. create a mysterious mood.

☐ b. introduce the reader to the topic of the article.

☐ c. compare Edwin Drake and John Townsend.

2. In this article, "They [local people] dubbed his project 'Colonel Drake's Folly'" means

☐ a. The local people wanted to sign up to serve under Colonel Drake.

☐ b. The local people didn't think the project had any chance of succeeding.

☐ c. The local people were kind to Drake.

3. Choose the statement below that best describes the author's position in paragraph 11.

☐ a. Drake got what he deserved since he had been careless about getting the patent.

☐ b. It is outrageous that just anyone can get a good pension from the state of Pennsylvania.

☐ c. It is sad that Drake didn't benefit from the oil boom he helped to create.

4. The author probably wrote this article in order to

☐ a. inform the reader about the person who drilled the first oil well.

☐ b. express an opinion about the careful use of natural resources.

☐ c. list the ways in which oil is used in the world today.

_____ Number of correct answers

Record your personal assessment of your work on the Critical Thinking Chart on page 74.

CRITICAL THINKING

Summarizing and Paraphrasing

Follow the directions provided for questions 1 and 2. Put an X in the box next to the correct answer for the other question.

1. Look for the important ideas and events in paragraphs 6 and 7. Summarize those paragraphs in one or two sentences.

_____

_____

_____

2. Complete the following one-sentence summary of the article using the lettered phrases from the phrase bank below. Write the letters on the lines.

> **Phrase Bank:**
> a. the first meeting of Edwin Drake and John Townsend
> b. Drake's death and a description of his monument
> c. all the ways that Drake tried to get oil

The article about Edwin Drake and the first oil well begins with _____, goes on to explain _____, and ends with _____.

3. Choose the sentence that correctly restates the following sentence from the article:

"The word of Drake's discovery touched off an oil boom as wild as any gold rush."

☐ a. When people learned about Drake's discovery, they started a gold rush.

☐ b. Drake's discovery of oil caused a wild oil boom similar to the one that happened after gold was discovered.

☐ c. After Drake said that he had discovered oil, the sound of the exploding oil well was heard by many people.

_____ Number of correct answers

Record your personal assessment of your work on the Critical Thinking Chart on page 74.

Critical Thinking

Follow the directions provided for questions 1, 3, and 4. Put an X in the box next to the correct answer for the other questions.

1. For each statement below, write O if it expresses an opinion or write F if it expresses a fact.

_____ a. Anyone could copy Drake's methods without paying him because he had no patent on them.

_____ b. Drake had to borrow money from friends to continue his project.

_____ c. The people of Titusville didn't deserve to become rich because they made so much fun of Edwin Drake.

CRITICAL THINKING

2. From the article, you can predict that if Drake had gotten a patent on his method, he

☐ a.   would have been rich.

☐ b.   would still have died poor.

☐ c.   would not be known as "Founder of the Petroleum Industry."

3. Choose from the letters below to correctly complete the following statement. Write the letters on the lines.

In the article, _____ and _____ were alike in their fascination with oil.

a.   Edwin Drake

b.   John Townsend

c.   the people of Titusville

4. Choose from the letters below to correctly complete the following statement. Write the letters on the lines.

According to the article, _____ caused people to _____, and the effect was _____.

a.   be able to collect oil easily

b.   many people became rich by collecting and selling the oil

c.   Drake's invention of the oil well

5. What did you have to do to answer question 1?

☐ a.   find an opinion (what someone thinks about something)

☐ b.   find a description (how something looks)

☐ c.   find an effect (something that happened)

_____ Number of correct answers

Record your personal assessment of your work on the Critical Thinking Chart on page 74.

Personal Response

I wonder why

_____

_____

_____

_____

Self-Assessment

Which concepts or ideas from the article were difficult to understand?

_____

_____

_____

_____

Which were easy to understand?

_____

_____

_____

_____

CRITICAL THINKING

A DIAMOND CALLED EUREKA

It all began by accident. Daniel Jacobs was tinkering with a water pipe on his farm near the hamlet of Hopetown, South Africa. The pipe had become clogged. Daniel needed a long, thin stick to clear out the pipe. He asked his young son, Erasmus, to fetch him one.

2 It was the spring of 1867. Erasmus looked about the pasture near the Orange River. At last he found a suitable branch. Then he decided to rest a moment under the shade of a tree. As he relaxed, his eye caught a twinkle in the grass. The light came from what looked like a shiny pebble or a stone which the sun seemed to hit just right. Curious, Erasmus walked over and picked it up. To him it was just another pretty pebble. He slipped it into the pocket of his corduroy suit. Later that day, Erasmus showed it to his sister, Louisa. She put it with the other pebbles they kept for use in a game called "Five Stones."

3 About a month later, a neighbor named Schalk van Niekirk dropped by while the children were playing this game. Seeing the stone, van Niekirk picked it up. As he wiped the dust off its surface, he saw the stone's wonderful glitter. Van Niekirk asked Mrs. Jacobs if he could buy the stone, but she just shook her head and laughed. To her, the pebble was nothing. She figured there must be millions of similar pebbles along the banks of the Orange River. She told van Niekirk he could ahead and keep the stone.

4 As van Niekirk took it, he had a vague notion that it might be worth something. A few days later, he sold it to an Irish peddler named John O'Reilly. O'Reilly didn't pay him much for it. So there is some question whether van Niekirk actually knew what he was selling. O'Reilly, on the other hand, felt certain he was getting a diamond.

5 O'Reilly took the stone to several store owners in Hopetown. They all dismissed it as worthless. "It is a pretty stone," said one. "It might even be topaz, but no one will pay anything for it." These business-people, apparently, didn't know a raw diamond when they saw one. O'Reilly next took it to the town of Colesberg. There a state official named Lorenzo Boyes tested the stone on a pane of glass. A diamond is hard enough to cut glass. And indeed, the stone easily etched out marks on the pane. "I believe it's a diamond," Boyes said.

6 O'Reilly was delighted to hear that. He offered to share any money he got for the diamond with Boyes. Dr. Kirsh, a pharmacist, happened to be in the room at the time. "Nonsense," he said, "I'll bet you a new hat it is only a topaz."

7 "It's a bet," responded Boyes.

8 Boyes sent the stone to Dr. W. Guybon Atherstone. He was the top mineralogist in South Africa. Surprisingly, Boyes didn't bother to take many precautions when he mailed it. He sent the stone by regular

Diamonds and gold are two minerals found in South Africa. This miner is working in a South African gold mine.

The Eureka Diamond (above) looked nothing like this when Erasmus Jacobs and his sister used it for the game "Five Stones."

mail in an unsealed envelope. When Atherstone opened the letter, the stone fell out and rolled across the floor. After picking it up, Atherstone examined it carefully. He then dashed off a note to Boyes, "I congratulate you on the stone you have sent me," he wrote. "It is a veritable diamond."

9   Boyes had won a new hat. The shiny pebble was a marvelous diamond. It weighed 21.25 carats. (One carat is a measure of weight equal to 200 milligrams.) When it was cut, the clear, blue-white stone was about the size of a sparrow's egg. O'Reilly sold the diamond for about $2,500. Later, the diamond was put on display in Paris, France. There it became known as the Eureka diamond. In the Greek language, *eureka* means "I have found it!"

10   At this time, South Africa was a British colony. It was a poor land filled mostly with farmers. The whole place seemed to be little more than a colonial backwater. Some people thought the discovery of the Eureka Diamond could change South Africa. Richard Southey, a South African official, certainly thought so. "This diamond is the rock upon which the future success of South Africa will be built," he said.

11   Others disagreed. After all, the occasional finding of a diamond had

happened before. It did not mean that there were others lying around. Besides, most people simply could not believe that the dry and dusty land of South Africa could yield diamonds. It just didn't look like diamond country. One expert said, "The geological character of that part of the country renders it impossible." Another claimed that the "discovery" was just a wild scheme to encourage more people to move to South Africa. One critic said that any diamonds found there must have been brought from some distant land. He even suggested that they had been carried to the Orange River in the "gizzards of ostriches."

12   For a couple of years, it appeared that the critics were right. Only a few more diamonds were found, and they were small. Then, in March of 1869, a shepherd outdid Erasmus Jacobs. He stumbled upon a magnificent white diamond of unmatched purity. The shepherd announced he would sell the diamond only if he got 500 sheep, 10 oxen, and a horse in return. To him, that seemed like a very high price. So he must have been shocked when a much shrewder Schalk van Niekerk happily agreed to the deal. This stone, when cut, turned out to be the famous "Star of South Africa." It weighed a whopping 83.50 carats.

13   That find, at last, silenced all the critics. More discoveries quickly followed. Soon the great South African diamond rush was on. Prospectors streamed in on foot, on horseback, and by wagon. By 1870, there were more than ten thousand diggers looking for the right kind of shiny pebbles. The true mineral wealth of South Africa became known when huge deposits of gold as well as diamonds were found. A little boy's shiny pebble had helped to change a poor country into one of the world's richest. It is true that the name "Eureka" was given only to the diamond found by young Erasmus Jacobs. But it could have been given just as easily to South Africa itself.

If you have been timed while reading this article, enter your reading time below. Then turn to the Words-per-Minute Table on page 71 and look up your reading speed (words per minute). Enter your reading speed on the graph on page 72.

Reading Time: Lesson 6

_____ : _____
Minutes   Seconds

A | Finding the Main Idea

One statement below expresses the main idea of the article. One statement is too general, or too broad. The other statement explains only part of the article; it is too narrow. Label the statements using the following key:

M—Main Idea   **B—Too Broad**   **N—Too Narrow**

_____ 1. John O'Reilly suspected that the glittering stone he bought was a diamond, but several store owners claimed it was worthless.

_____ 2. Diamonds had a tremendous impact on South Africa.

_____ 3. The discovery of a large diamond set off a diamond rush in South Africa and contributed to that country's reputation for mineral wealth.

_____ Score 15 points for a correct M answer.

_____ Score 5 points for each correct B or N answer.

_____ **Total Score:** Finding the Main Idea

B | Recalling Facts

How well do you remember the facts in the article? Put an X in the box next to the answer that correctly completes each statement about the article.

1. The Eureka diamond was first found by
   - ☐ a. Schalk van Niekirk.
   - ☐ b. Erasmus Jacobs.
   - ☐ c. John O'Reilly.

2. The Jacobs children used the stone
   - ☐ a. to make their family rich.
   - ☐ b. to complete their rock collection.
   - ☐ c. in a game called "Five Stones."

3. Lorenzo Boyes decided that the stone might be a diamond after he
   - ☐ a. saw that it could scratch glass.
   - ☐ b. looked at it through a magnifying glass.
   - ☐ c. weighed it on a sensitive scale.

4. The Eureka Diamond weighs about
   - ☐ a. 21.25 carats.
   - ☐ b. 59.75 carats.
   - ☐ c. 83.50 carats.

5. The diamond rush in South Africa took place around
   - ☐ a. 1805.
   - ☐ b. 1870.
   - ☐ c. 1922.

_____ Score 5 points for each correct answer.

_____ **Total Score:** Recalling Facts

C | Making Inferences

When you combine your own experience and information from a text to draw a conclusion that is not directly stated in that text, you are making an inference. Below are five statements that may or may not be inferences based on information in the article. Label the statements using the following key:

C—Correct Inference   **F—Faulty Inference**

_____ 1. Even after he studied it, Lorenzo Boyes was not absolutely sure that the stone Erasmus Jacobs found was a diamond.

_____ 2. It is quite common to find large diamonds lying on the ground in South Africa.

_____ 3. If you bought the Eureka Diamond today, you would pay more than $2500.

_____ 4. South African officials were pleased when diamonds were found in their country.

_____ 5. In 1867, any diamond that was found in South Africa became the property of the colony itself, not of the person who found it.

Score 5 points for each correct answer.

_____ **Total Score:** Making Inferences

D | Using Words Precisely

Each numbered sentence below contains an underlined word or phrase from the article. Following the sentence are three definitions. One definition is closest to the meaning of the underlined word. One definition is opposite or nearly opposite. Label those two definitions using the following key. Do not label the remaining definition.

C—Closest   **O—Opposite or Nearly Opposite**

1. Daniel Jacobs was tinkering with a water pipe on his farm near the hamlet of Hopetown, South Africa.

_____ a. huge city

_____ b. capital

_____ c. small village

2. At last he found a suitable branch.

_____ a. not appropriate

_____ b. thin

_____ c. acceptable

3. As van Niekirk took it, he had a vague notion that it might be worth something.

_____ a. fuzzy, indistinct

_____ b. clear

_____ c. happy

4. "It is a veritable diamond."

_____ a. fake

_____ b. true

_____ c. beautiful

5. After all, the <u>occasional</u> finding of a diamond had happened before.

_____ a. every now and then

_____ b. constant

_____ c. lucky

_____ Score 3 points for each correct C answer.

_____ Score 2 points for each correct O answer.

_____ **Total Score:** Using Words Precisely

Enter the four total scores in the spaces below, and add them together to find your Reading Comprehension Score. Then record your score on the graph on page 73.

Score	Question Type	Lesson 6
_____	Finding the Main Idea	
_____	Recalling Facts	
_____	Making Inferences	
_____	Using Words Precisely	
_____	**Reading Comprehension Score**	

Author's Approach

Put an X in the box next to the correct answer.

1. The author uses the first sentence of the article to

☐ a. inform the reader about living conditions in South Africa.

☐ b. entertain the reader with a joke about the Eureka Diamond.

☐ c. appeal to the reader's curiosity about the accident.

2. Which of the following statements from the article best describes the Eureka diamond as Erasmus Jacobs first saw it?

☐ a. "The light came from what looked like a shiny pebble or a stone which the sun seemed to hit just right."

☐ b. "To her, the pebble was nothing."

☐ c. "When it was cut, the clear, blue-white stone was about the size of a sparrow's egg."

3. What does the author imply by saying "Surprisingly, Boyes didn't bother to take many precautions when he mailed it [the stone]"?

☐ a. Boyes didn't have enough money to mail the stone in a safe way.

☐ b. In South Africa, there was no reliable method of sending valuable objects.

☐ c. Boyes was not absolutely certain that the stone was a diamond.

4. The author tells this story mainly by

☐ a. relating events in the order they happened.

☐ b. comparing different topics.

☐ c. using his or her imagination and creativity.

_____ Number of correct answers

Record your personal assessment of your work on the Critical Thinking Chart on page 74.

CRITICAL THINKING

Summarizing and Paraphrasing

Follow the directions provided for question 1. Put an X in the box next to the correct answer for question 2.

1. Look for the important ideas and events in paragraphs 12 and 13. Summarize those paragraphs in one or two sentences.

_____

_____

_____

2. Read the statement about the article below. Then read the paraphrase of that statement. Choose the reason that best tells why the paraphrase does not say the same thing as the statement.

    Statement: Some critics claimed that the discovery of the Eureka Diamond was just a scheme to get more people to move to South Africa.

    Paraphrase: Some people said that the discovery of the Eureka Diamond discouraged people from moving to South Africa.

    ☐ a. Paraphrase says too much.

    ☐ b. Paraphrase doesn't say enough.

    ☐ c. Paraphrase doesn't agree with the statement about the article.

    _____ Number of correct answers

    Record your personal assessment of your work on the Critical Thinking Chart on page 74.

Critical Thinking

Follow the directions provided for questions 1 and 3. Put an X in the box next to the correct answer for the other questions.

1. For each statement below, write O if it expresses an opinion or write F if it expresses a fact.

    _____ a. Erasmus Jacobs found the Eureka Diamond in 1867.

    _____ b. Diamonds are the most beautiful of all the gems.

    _____ c. In 1867, most residents of South Africa were farmers.

2. Considering Schalk van Niekerk's actions as told in this article, you can conclude that he

    ☐ a. knew that the Star of South Africa was worth more than the shepherd was asking for it.

    ☐ b. disliked the shepherd who found the Star of South Africa.

    ☐ c. was a wealthy man.

3. Choose from the letters below to correctly complete the following statement. Write the letters on the lines.

    On the positive side, _____, but on the negative side _____.

    a. a diamond is hard enough to cut glass.

    b. the people who found the Eureka Diamond and the Star of South Africa did not get much in return for finding the valuable stones

    c. people are now able to enjoy the beauty of the Eureka Diamond and the Star of South Africa

4. What did you have to do to answer question 3?

☐ a.   find an opinion (what someone thinks about something)

☐ b.   find a description (how something looks)

☐ c.   find a contrast (how things are different)

_____ Number of correct answers

Record your personal assessment of your work on the Critical Thinking Chart on page 74.

Personal Response

What new question do you have about this topic?

_____

_____

_____

_____

While reading the article, I found it easiest to

_____

_____

_____

_____

AFRICAN ADVENTURE
Seeking the Source of the Nile

They were a formidable couple, Florence and Samuel Baker. She was tactful and charming. He was forceful and ambitious. Both were gutsy and determined explorers. When they made up their minds to do something, they did it.

2   In 1861, the Bakers decided to find the source of the Nile, the world's longest river. Since ancient times, the source had remained a riddle that no one could solve. If anyone could find the source, however, it was the Bakers. Samuel Baker said that he could think of nothing in this world that could "resist a determined will."

3   The search was not a journey to be taken lightly. It took time, lots of money, and careful planning. The Bakers spent 14 months in Khartoum, the capital of the Sudan, just getting ready. They studied Arabic and local customs. They bought the guns, food, boats, pack animals, clothes, and other equipment they needed. Also, they signed up nearly 100 porters and soldiers to come with them. At last, on December 18, 1862, they set sail up the Nile.

4   Their first destination was Gondokoro. This village was about 1,000 miles up the

Although the Bakers thought Lake Albert was the source of the Nile River, Lake Victoria (pictured here) is the Nile's true source.

river in southern Sudan. Getting there was not easy. For 500 miles they saw nothing but desert on both sides of the Nile. Then they had to sail through a vast, steamy, mosquito-ridden swamp known as the Sudd. "It is not surprising," Samuel Baker later wrote, "that the ancients gave up the exploration of the Nile when they came to the [Sudd]."

5   On February 2, 1863, they reached Gondokoro. The village was a slave-trading center. The sight of men, women, and children being sold nauseated the Bakers. But as strangers in a strange land, they were powerless to stop it. And, in any case, their prime goal was to find the source of the Nile. (Seven years later, however, Samuel was named governor of the region. During his four-year term, he and Florence fought hard to end the slave trade.)

6   Gondokoro was like a gold rush town in the Wild West. Slave traders often got drunk and fired their guns in the air. Despite the hostile atmosphere, the Bakers kept their cool. Once, a member of their own expedition complained bitterly about the food. It looked as if he might incite a full-scale mutiny. Samuel punched the man and knocked him down. Some of the man's friends then threatened to beat up Samuel. Florence, who was nearby in bed with a fever, rushed to his aid. Her sudden appearance took the angry men by total

surprise. They had apparently never seen a woman act so boldly. Out of respect, the men backed off. Calmly, Florence asked Samuel to forgive the ringleader. He did and the crisis passed.

7   On February 15, the Bakers suffered a bitter disappointment. John Speke arrived in the village from the south. He, too, had been looking for the source of the Nile and he now announced that he had found it. Speke claimed that the great river began at Lake Victoria. He had trekked deep into the wilderness to find this huge lake. Local wars, dwindling supplies, and his own weariness kept him from following the river that flowed out of the lake. Still, Speke was sure it was the Nile. And he had gotten to its source first.

8   Discouraged but not willing to give up, the Bakers decided to explore the parts of the Nile that Speke had missed. This area included an uncharted lake known to the natives as Luta N'zige. The natives said that it was only two weeks away. But the trip to Luta N'zige would take the Bakers much longer than two weeks.

9   Florence and Samuel left Gondokoro in March. They ran into trouble almost from the start. The hilly terrain was treacherous. Also, the Bakers had no maps of this unexplored territory. Civil wars slowed their march. Food supplies ran low and both Florence and Samuel fell sick. Though often hungry, they turned down

the chance to eat a decomposed boar's head filled with maggots. In order to keep going, the Bakers had no choice but to join a slave trader's caravan. The idea rankled the Bakers. Samuel said that slave traders turned "every country into a wasp's nest."

10   In January 1864, they arrived in the Kingdom of Bunyoro. It had taken them

Sir Samuel and Lady Baker in an undated engraving

more than nine months to get this far. The Bakers and Kamrasi, the ruler of the kingdom, exchanged some gifts. What the Bakers really wanted, however, was more guides and porters. What Kamrasi wanted was Florence. He wanted to add her to his harem. "I will send you to the lake," he said, "but, *you must leave your wife with me!*" Angrily, Samuel pulled his gun and pointed it at Kamrasi.

11   At this point, Florence rose from her seat and spoke firmly to Kamrasi in Arabic. It was a brilliant move. Kamrasi didn't understand a word, but he got the message that Florence was not available. Politely, Kamrasi explained that he had meant no offense. Since he was willing to give Samuel one of his wives, he hadn't realized that Samuel would object to giving up Florence.

12   Soon thereafter, the Bakers were able to resume their journey to Luta N'zige. But once again they ran into trouble. Florence, suffering from extreme sunstroke, slipped into a coma. The porters had to carry her on a litter. After a few days, Florence came out of her coma. But she was delirious. For hours she ranted wildly. Samuel felt certain that Florence was dying. He told his men to prepare a grave for his wife. It turned out that was not necessary. Miraculously, Florence recovered. She awoke the next day with eyes "calm and clear."

13   On March 14, 1864, the party at last reached Luta N'zige. Samuel rushed up ahead. Eager to see the lake, he climbed up a high ridge. He later wrote, "The glory of our prize burst suddenly upon me! There, like a sea of quicksilver, lay far beneath the grand expense of water, a boundless sea horizon...."

14   Samuel renamed the body of water Lake Albert, in honor of Queen Victoria's late husband. Florence, holding onto Samuel's shoulder, hobbled to the shore. She stood with her ankles in the water. They had reached their destination. It was a glorious moment. "No European foot had ever trod upon its sand," Samuel later wrote. "Nor had the eyes of a white man ever scanned its vast expanse of water. We were the first."

15   Baker was convinced that Lake Albert, not Lake Victoria, was the true source of the Nile. "[Lake Albert] was the key to the great secret that even Julius Caesar yearned to unravel, but in vain," he proclaimed. On this count, Samuel was wrong. Lake Albert wasn't the main source of the Nile. Speke's theory about Lake Victoria was correct. But it would not be proven for years to come.

16   The Bakers were not finished yet. They had to make it back to Gondokoro. Along the way, they suffered many more hard-ships. Food was again in short supply. At times they had to eat crocodile flesh. Samuel said it was the worst meat he had ever eaten. It tasted like a combination of "bad fish, rotten flesh, and musk." A storm on Lake Albert nearly capsized their canoe.

17   A short time later, the Bakers discovered a huge 130-foot waterfall on the Nile. Samuel named it Murchison Falls after a geographer friend. Their awe was short-lived, however. A giant bull hippo attacked their canoe, lifting it half out of the water. At the same time, more than a dozen crocodiles began to circle the canoe, hoping for a feast. "Fine fun it would have been for these monsters," wrote Samuel later, "had the bull hippo been successful in his attempt to capsize us."

18   The Bakers finally made it back to Gondokoro in February 1865. There were no Europeans to greet them. Florence and Samuel had long ago been given up for dead. The only thing the village had to offer was bubonic plague. So the Bakers fled back to the Nile. They reached Khartoum on May 5.

19   For his discoveries, the Royal Geo-graphical Society gave Samuel its Victoria Gold Medal. But Samuel knew who else deserved the medal. He later wrote about "a devoted companion of my pilgrimage to whom I owed success and life—my wife."

If you have been timed while reading this article, enter your reading time below. Then turn to the Words-per-Minute Table on page 71 and look up your reading speed (words per minute). Enter your reading speed on the graph on page 72.

Reading Time: Lesson 7

_____ : _____
Minutes   Seconds

A | Finding the Main Idea

One statement below expresses the main idea of the article. One statement is too general, or too broad. The other statement explains only part of the article; it is too narrow. Label the statements using the following key:

M—Main Idea   **B—Too Broad**   **N—Too Narrow**

_____ 1. Samuel and Florence Baker were disgusted to see men, women, and children being sold into slavery.

_____ 2. The 19th century was an age of exploration in Africa.

_____ 3. Florence and Samuel Baker were fearless explorers of Africa who spent years searching for the source of the Nile River.

_____ Score 15 points for a correct M answer.

_____ Score 5 points for each correct B or N answer.

_____ **Total Score:** Finding the Main Idea

B | Recalling Facts

How well do you remember the facts in the article? Put an X in the box next to the answer that correctly completes each statement about the article.

1. The Bakers spent 14 months preparing for their search for the source of the Nile
   - ☐ a. in Khartoum.
   - ☐ b. in Gondokoro.
   - ☐ c. near Bunyoro.

2. In 1870, Samuel Baker was named
   - ☐ a. mayor of Khartoum.
   - ☐ b. governor of the Gondokoro region.
   - ☐ c. a general of the British army in Africa.

3. The first European to locate the source of the Nile was
   - ☐ a. Florence Baker.
   - ☐ b. Samuel Baker.
   - ☐ c. John Speke.

4. The ruler of Bunyoro surprised the Bakers when he
   - ☐ a. fed them a boar's head filled with maggots.
   - ☐ b. wanted to add Florence to his harem.
   - ☐ c. prepared a grave for Florence.

5. For his discoveries, Samuel was awarded
   - ☐ a. the Victoria Gold Medal.
   - ☐ b. the Congressional Medal of Honor.
   - ☐ c. knighthood.

Score 5 points for each correct answer.

_____ **Total Score:** Recalling Facts

C | Making Inferences

When you combine your own experience and information from a text to draw a conclusion that is not directly stated in that text, you are making an inference. Below are five statements that may or may not be inferences based on information in the article. Label the statements using the following key:

C—Correct Inference   F—Faulty Inference

_____ 1. People back home were impressed when they heard the Bakers' stories about their adventures in Africa.

_____ 2. Samuel was a peace-loving man who never raised his hand against any other human being.

_____ 3. Florence did not always follow the rules society's rules for women.

_____ 4. Florence probably had to persuade Samuel to accompany her on her search for the source of the Nile.

_____ 5. During the 19th century, women were not routinely given medals by the Royal Geographical Society, no matter what they had accomplished.

Score 5 points for each correct answer.

_____ **Total Score:** Making Inferences

D | Using Words Precisely

Each numbered sentence below contains an underlined word or phrase from the article. Following the sentence are three definitions. One definition is closest to the meaning of the underlined word. One definition is opposite or nearly opposite. Label those two definitions using the following key. Do not label the remaining definition.

C—Closest   O—Opposite or Nearly Opposite

1. They were a <u>formidable</u> couple, Florence and Samuel Baker.

_____ a. elderly

_____ b. pathetic

_____ c. awe-inspiring

2. It looked as if he might <u>incite</u> a full-scale mutiny.

_____ a. prevent

_____ b. encourage

_____ c. observe

3. The hilly terrain was <u>treacherous</u>.

_____ a. dangerous

_____ b. lovely

_____ c. safe

4. The idea <u>rankled</u> the Bakers.

_____ a. surprised

_____ b. annoyed

_____ c. pleased

5. After a few days, Florence came out of her coma. But she was <u>delirious</u>.

_____ a. mentally confused

_____ b. angry

_____ c. clear-headed

_____ Score 3 points for each correct C answer.

_____ Score 2 points for each correct O answer.

_____ **Total Score:** Using Words Precisely

Enter the four total scores in the spaces below, and add them together to find your Reading Comprehension Score. Then record your score on the graph on page 73.

Score	Question Type	Lesson 7
_____	Finding the Main Idea	
_____	Recalling Facts	
_____	Making Inferences	
_____	Using Words Precisely	
_____	**Reading Comprehension Score**	

Author's Approach

Put an X in the box next to the correct answer.

1. The main purpose of the first paragraph is to

☐ a. introduce and describe the Bakers.

☐ b. describe the Bakers' search for the Nile.

☐ c. create a peaceful mood.

2. What is the author's purpose in writing "African Adventure: Seeking the Source of the Nile"?

☐ a. To encourage the reader to save endangered species

☐ b. To express an opinion about European exploration of Africa

☐ c. To inform the reader about two determined explorers

3. From the statements below, choose those that you believe the author would agree with.

☐ a. Florence and Samuel were equally brave.

☐ b. Florence deserved the Victoria Gold Medal as much as Samuel did.

☐ c. The Bakers purposely tried to deceive others into believing they had found the true source of the Nile.

_____ Number of correct answers

Record your personal assessment of your work on the Critical Thinking Chart on page 74.

Summarizing and Paraphrasing

Put an X in the box next to the correct answer for question 1. Follow the directions provided for question 2.

1. Below are summaries of the article. Choose the summary that says all the most important things about the article but in the fewest words.

☐ a. Florence and Samuel Baker were discouraged when they found out that John Speke had supposedly found the source of the Nile. Even so, they continued their search, spending over a year at it. They suffered illness, and at one time, it seemed as if Florence were going to die of extreme sunstroke. Finally, they found Lake Albert which they believed was the source. Unfortunately, they were mistaken.

☐ b. Even though Florence and Samuel Baker did not find the source of the Nile, they showed great courage in exploring parts of Africa that had never been seen by any white person before.

☐ c. Many people searched for the source of the Nile, including Florence and Samuel Baker and John Speke.

2. Reread paragraph 18 in the article. Below, write a summary of the paragraph in no more than 25 words.

_____

_____

_____

_____

Reread your summary and decide whether it covers the important ideas in the paragraph. Next, decide how to shorten the summary to 15 words or less without leaving out any essential information. Write this summary below.

_____

_____

_____

_____ Number of correct answers

Record your personal assessment of your work on the Critical Thinking Chart on page 74.

Critical Thinking

Put an X in the box next to the correct answer for questions 1, 2, 4, and 5. Follow the directions provided for question 3.

1. Which of the following statements from the article is an opinion rather than a fact?

☐ a. "At last, on December 18, 1982, they [the Bakers] set sail up the Nile."

☐ b. "They were a formidable couple, Florence and Samuel Baker."

☐ c. "Food supplies ran low and both Florence and Samuel fell sick."

2. From what Samuel said, you can predict that if it had been possible, he would have

☐ a. claimed all the credit for the explorations that both he and Florence had done.

☐ b. given back the Victoria Gold Medal.

☐ c. shared the Victoria Gold Medal with his wife.

3. Read paragraph 5. Then choose from the letters below to correctly complete the following statement. Write the letters on the lines.

According to paragraph 5, _____ because _____.

a. they saw people being sold into slavery

b. the Bakers felt nauseated

c. the Bakers named a lake they found for Queen Victoria's husband

4. How are the adventures of the Bakers related to the theme of this book?

☐ a. The Bakers found things that had never been seen by Europeans before.

☐ b. The Bakers learned to speak Arabic.

☐ c. Samuel Baker won an important award for his adventures.

5. What did you have to do to answer question 1?

☐ a. find an opinion (what someone thinks about something)

☐ b. find a description (how something looks)

☐ c. find a definition (what something means)

_____ Number of correct answers

Record your personal assessment of your work on the Critical Thinking Chart on page 74.

Personal Response

A question I would like answered by Florence Baker is

_____

_____

_____

_____

Self-Assessment

The part I found most difficult about the article was

_____

_____

_____

_____

I found this difficult because

_____

_____

_____

_____

CRITICAL THINKING

Compare and Contrast

Think about the articles you have read in Unit One. Pick the four individuals that you think contributed the most to humankind. Write the titles of the articles about them in the first column of the chart below. Use information you learned from the articles to fill in the empty boxes of the chart.

Title	What did this person invent or discover?	How did this invention or discovery affect other people?	Did people realize the importance of his or her work at the time?

The person I think contributed most to the world is _____ because _____

_____

_____

Words-per-Minute Table

Unit One

Directions: If you were timed while reading an article, refer to the Reading Time you recorded in the box at the end of the article. Use this words-per-minute table to determine your reading speed for that article. Then plot your reading speed on the graph on page 72.

Lesson No. of Words	Sample 870	1 891	2 958	3 1225	4 1070	5 1004	6 1054	7 1401	
1:30	580	594	639	817	713	669	703	934	**90**
1:40	522	535	575	735	642	602	632	841	**100**
1:50	475	486	523	668	584	548	575	764	**110**
2:00	435	446	479	613	535	502	527	701	**120**
2:10	402	411	442	565	494	463	486	647	**130**
2:20	373	382	411	525	459	430	452	600	**140**
2:30	348	356	383	490	428	402	422	560	**150**
2:40	326	334	359	459	401	377	395	525	**160**
2:50	307	314	338	432	378	354	372	494	**170**
3:00	290	297	319	408	357	335	351	467	**180**
3:10	275	281	303	387	338	317	333	442	**190**
3:20	261	267	287	368	321	301	316	420	**200**
3:30	249	255	274	350	306	287	301	400	**210**
3:40	237	243	261	334	292	274	287	382	**220**
3:50	227	232	250	320	279	262	275	365	**230**
4:00	218	223	240	306	268	251	264	350	**240**
4:10	209	214	230	294	257	241	253	336	**250**
4:20	201	206	221	283	247	232	243	323	**260**
4:30	193	198	213	272	238	223	234	311	**270**
4:40	186	191	205	263	229	215	226	300	**280**
4:50	180	184	198	253	221	208	218	290	**290**
5:00	174	178	192	245	214	201	211	280	**300**
5:10	168	172	185	237	207	194	204	271	**310**
5:20	163	167	180	230	201	188	198	263	**320**
5:30	158	162	174	223	195	183	192	255	**330**
5:40	154	157	169	216	189	177	186	247	**340**
5:50	149	153	164	210	183	172	181	240	**350**
6:00	145	149	160	204	178	167	176	234	**360**
6:10	141	144	155	199	174	163	171	227	**370**
6:20	137	141	151	193	169	159	166	221	**380**
6:30	134	137	147	188	165	154	162	216	**390**
6:40	131	134	144	184	161	151	158	210	**400**
6:50	127	130	140	179	157	147	154	205	**410**
7:00	124	127	137	175	153	143	151	200	**420**
7:10	121	124	134	171	149	140	147	195	**430**
7:20	119	122	131	167	146	137	144	191	**440**
7:30	116	119	128	163	143	134	141	187	**450**
7:40	113	116	125	160	140	131	137	183	**460**
7:50	111	114	122	156	137	128	135	179	**470**
8:00	109	111	120	153	134	126	132	175	**480**

Minutes and Seconds

Seconds

Plotting Your Progress: Reading Speed

Unit One

Directions: If you were timed while reading an article, write your words-per-minute rate for that article in the box under the number of the lesson. Then plot your reading speed on the graph by putting a small X on the line directly above the number of the lesson, across from the number of words per minute you read. As you mark your speed for each lesson, graph your progress by drawing a line to connect the X's.

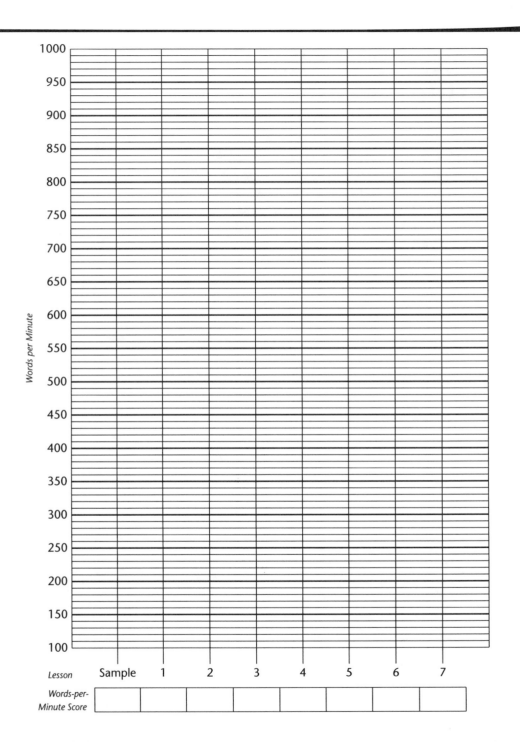

Plotting Your Progress: Reading Comprehension

Unit One

Directions: Write your Reading Comprehension score for each lesson in the box under the number of the lesson. Then plot your score on the graph by putting a small X on the line directly above the number of the lesson and across from the score you earned. As you mark your score for each lesson, graph your progress by drawing a line to connect the X's.

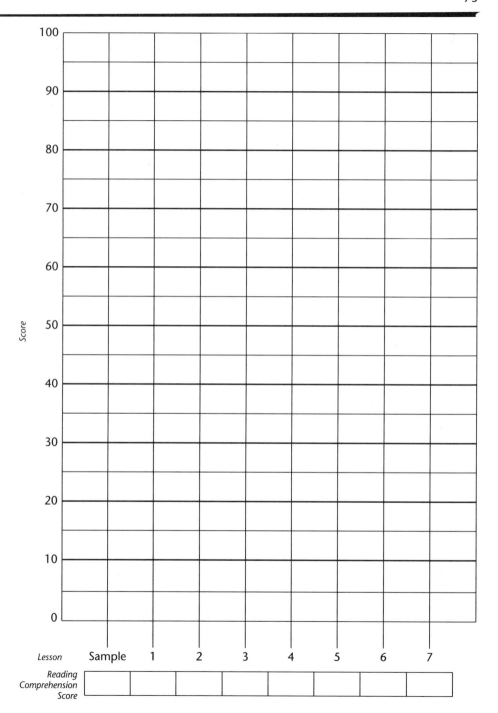

Score

Lesson	Sample	1	2	3	4	5	6	7
Reading Comprehension Score								

Plotting Your Progress: Critical Thinking

Unit One

Directions: Work with your teacher to evaluate your responses to the Critical Thinking questions for each lesson. Then fill in the appropriate spaces in the chart below. For each lesson and each type of Critical Thinking question, do the following: Mark a minus sign (–) in the box to indicate areas in which you feel you could improve. Mark a plus sign (+) to indicate areas in which you feel you did well. Mark a minus-slash-plus sign (–/+) to indicate areas in which you had mixed success. Then write any comments you have about your performance, including ideas for improvement.

Lesson	Author's Approach	Summarizing and Paraphrasing	Critical Thinking
Sample			
1			
2			
3			
4			
5			
6			
7			

UNIT TWO

THE EMPEROR AND HIS ARMY

For centuries the Chinese people lived with seemingly endless civil wars. Most couldn't recall a time when one group wasn't at some other group's throat. There was no political union. In fact, there was no country of China at all. Instead, there were seven separate Chinese states waging war to dominate each other. No state ever got strong enough to rule all the others, and the bloodshed went on and on.

2 This frustrating situation changed when a king called Qin Shi Huangdi came onto the scene. Qin Shi Huangdi (pronounced Chin Sure Wang-dee) became the leader of the state of Qin in 246 B.C. At the time he was crowned king, he was only 13 years old. He was too young to govern in his own right. So another man called a regent made all the decisions until the king turned 21.

3 When Qin finally got full power, he ruled with an iron will. For more than 16 years he waged war against the other Chinese states. At last, Qin achieved what no one else had done. He defeated all other Chinese states. And so in 221 B.C., Qin Shi Huangdi declared himself emperor of a unified China.

Qin Shi Huangdi's terra cotta army protected his tomb for 2,200 years before it was discovered by local peasants digging a well. The inset photo (upper left) shows a close-up of the army.

4 Qin ruled only 11 years, dying when he was 49 years old. Still, his reign was marked by incredible achievements and stunning cruelty. Under him, workers completed the Great Wall of China. This 1,500-mile wall was meant to keep out all foreigners, whom the Chinese called "barbarians." Qin also set up a uniform code of laws. He created a single currency and a single form of writing. And he created one system for weights and

measures. All of these changes would remain in place until the 20th century.

5 Qin had his dark side, to be sure. He was what we today might call a "control freak." Anyone who angered or displeased him was buried alive. Many people were executed this way during Qin's reign. He even tried to control the nonhuman world. Once, while he was on a visit to a famous mountain, a violent storm blew up and he had to turn back. Blaming the

The Great Wall of China stretches for 1,500 miles across northern China.

mountain for the storm, Qin ordered 3,000 workers to cut down all its trees. Then he told them to paint the mountain red—the color worn by prisoners.

6   Even as a young man, Qin had a morbid fear of death. In time, his fear turned into an obsession. He wouldn't be happy with just a long life; what he really craved was immortality. So he sent out some men to discover the fountain of youth. They didn't find it, of course. One minister then advised Qin to sleep in different places from time to time. In this way, the minister said, the emperor could avoid evil spirits that might be lurking about. Acting on his minister's advice, Qin had workers build covered passageways to connect his many palaces. Using these walkways, he could secretly move from one palace to another. Anyone who revealed his whereabouts was put to death.

7   If he couldn't live forever in this world, Emperor Qin wanted to take no chances on the next one. So he had a massive tomb built for himself. He began the tomb as soon as he became king of Qin. It wasn't shaped like the giant pyramids of ancient Egypt, but it was just as impressive. He had his future resting place buried under a mound of earth 15 stories high called Mount Li. At times, he had more than 700,000 men working on the tomb.

8   Like the Egyptian pharaohs, Qin wanted to ensure his happiness in the afterlife, so he told builders to put in everything he might need. They put in gold and jade jewelry. They stocked his

tomb with silks and fine clothes. For light, the workers added candles fueled with whale oil. Qin even decorated his tomb to look like a miniature version of China. The ceiling displayed drawings of the sky, and the floor was covered with drawings of the earth. In addition, all of China's rivers were reproduced in quicksilver. Qin even had water pumped in so his world would have its own "ocean."

9   But those luxuries weren't enough to please Qin. Even though he would be dead, Qin wanted to protect himself from an attack. Although he had defeated all the warring states, he still had enemies. If they ever decided to attack, Qin felt certain that they would approach from the east. So he created his own private army facing east to guard his tomb.

10   This was no toy army. Carved in a special clay called terra cotta, the 8,000 soldiers were full-size adults, each about six feet tall. Since each one was modeled on a real man, all of them had distinct facial features and hair styles. They also had individual expressions. Some looked fierce. Others looked proud and confident. And a few even looked as if they were about to smile. These men held real weapons—razor-sharp and ready for battle. The war chariots were real war chariots. The clay chariot horses were also life-size and beautiful. This huge army was buried along with Qin Shi Huangdi in 210 B.C. Over the centuries, the tomb was forgotten.

11   Now fast-forward nearly 2,200 years. In 1974, some peasants were digging a well about a mile from Mount Li. They

didn't find any water. But to their astonishment, they uncovered some of Qin's pottery army. The discovery shocked even the experts on China. No one thought that such a treasure could lie undetected for so long.

12   "Nothing compares with it," said one researcher. "There has never been [anything] of this scope and size anywhere in the world. Previous discoveries do not compare with this lot."

13   Others were impressed by the artistry. "I have rarely seen such sophisticated figures for a period as early as this."

14   The discovery altered history's view of Qin Shi Huangdi. For more than 2,000 years, he had been viewed as a cruel tyrant. Now scholars started to see his good points, as well. They began to credit him for ending China's civil wars and for uniting China. They also saw that his reign had produced some of the most spectacular art ever found.

If you have been timed while reading this article, enter your reading time below. Then turn to the Words-per-Minute Table on page 133 and look up your reading speed (words per minute). Enter your reading speed on the graph on page 134.

Reading Time: Lesson 8

_____ : _____
Minutes   Seconds

A | Finding the Main Idea

One statement below expresses the main idea of the article. One statement is too general, or too broad. The other statement explains only part of the article; it is too narrow. Label the statements using the following key:

M—Main Idea   **B—Too Broad**   **N—Too Narrow**

_____ 1. Emperor Qin Shi Huangdi's workers stocked his tomb with gold jewelry.

_____ 2. Emperor Qin Shi Huangdi is credited with uniting the warring Chinese, developing ways to manage the country, and sponsoring the creation of beautiful art.

_____ 3. Emperor Qin Shi Huangdi was an unusual ruler.

_____ Score 15 points for a correct M answer.

_____ Score 5 points for each correct B or N answer.

_____ **Total Score:** Finding the Main Idea

B | Recalling Facts

How well do you remember the facts in the article? Put an X in the box next to the answer that correctly completes each statement about the article.

1. Qin Shi Huangdi came into power when he was
    ☐ a. 13 years old.
    ☐ b. 11 years old.
    ☐ c. 18 years old.

2. Qin defeated
    ☐ a. Japan.
    ☐ b. Korean invaders.
    ☐ c. all the other Chinese states.

3. Under Qin's rule, workers completed the
    ☐ a. Trans-Siberian Railroad.
    ☐ b. Great Wall of China.
    ☐ c. pyramids.

4. Outside Qin's tomb was
    ☐ a. a pack of fierce dogs.
    ☐ b. an army of clay soldiers.
    ☐ c. a deep moat filled with water.

5. Qin's tomb was located
    ☐ a. under Mount Li.
    ☐ b. beneath his palace.
    ☐ c. in a building that was 15 stories high.

Score 5 points for each correct answer.

_____ **Total Score:** Recalling Facts

Making Inferences

When you combine your own experience and information from a text to draw a conclusion that is not directly stated in that text, you are making an inference. Below are five statements that may or may not be inferences based on information in the article. Label the statements using the following key:

C—Correct Inference   F—Faulty Inference

_____ 1. Qin was forever grateful to the regent who ruled in his place until Qin was 21.

_____ 2. To build the Great Wall, Qin needed the help of a great many workers.

_____ 3. Qin was always able to control his own emotions.

_____ 4. All the people ruled by Qin loved and respected him.

_____ 5. Qin was a creative and forceful leader.

Score 5 points for each correct answer.

_____ **Total Score:** Making Inferences

D **Using Words Precisely**

Each numbered sentence below contains an underlined word or phrase from the article. Following the sentence are three definitions. One definition is closest to the meaning of the underlined word. One definition is opposite or nearly opposite. Label those two definitions using the following key. Do not label the remaining definition.

C—Closest   O—Opposite or Nearly Opposite

1. Instead, there were seven separate Chinese states waging war to dominate each other.

_____ a. rule

_____ b. be controlled by

_____ c. imitate

2. Even as a young man, Qin had a morbid fear of death.

_____ a. cheerful and healthy

_____ b. complicated

_____ c. gloomy and unwholesome

3. Qin even decorated his tomb to look like a miniature version of China.

_____ a. over-sized

_____ b. realistic

_____ c. tiny

4. No one thought that such a treasure could lie undetected for so long.

_____ a. underground

_____ b. hidden

_____ c. obvious

5. "I have rarely seen such <u>sophisticated</u> figures for a period as early as this."

_____ a. advanced

_____ b. simple

_____ c. appealing

_____ Score 3 points for each correct C answer.

_____ Score 2 points for each correct O answer.

_____ **Total Score:** Using Words Precisely

Enter the four total scores in the spaces below, and add them together to find your Reading Comprehension Score. Then record your score on the graph on page 135.

Score	Question Type	Lesson 8
_____	Finding the Main Idea	
_____	Recalling Facts	
_____	Making Inferences	
_____	Using Words Precisely	
_____	**Reading Comprehension Score**	

Author's Approach

Put an X in the box next to the correct answer.

1. What does the author mean by the statement in paragraph 1 "In fact, there was no country of China at all"?

☐ a. The land area we call China had not yet emerged from the sea.

☐ b. There was no single nation to which all the people in the area felt that they belonged.

☐ c. No one lived in the area we call China.

2. The main purpose of the first paragraph is to

☐ a. express an opinion about the horrors of war.

☐ b. inform the reader about Qin's personality.

☐ c. describe the situation in China before Qin.

3. Choose the statement below that is the weakest argument for believing that Qin was a great ruler.

☐ a. When Qin lost his temper, he cruelly punished people and sometimes even punished things.

☐ b. Qin supervised the building of the Great Wall of China.

☐ c. Qin created a workable system of weights and measures.

4. The author probably wrote this article in order to

☐ a. inform the reader about an interesting and unusual ruler.

☐ b. encourage the reader to travel around the world.

☐ c. persuade the reader to become an archaeologist.

_____ Number of correct answers

Record your personal assessment of your work on the Critical Thinking Chart on page 136.

CRITICAL THINKING

Summarizing and Paraphrasing

Follow the directions provided for questions 1 and 2. Put an X in the box next to the correct answer for question 3.

1. Complete the following one-sentence summary of the article using the lettered phrases from the phrase bank below. Write the letters on the lines.

> **Phrase Bank:**
> a. Qin's accomplishments as emperor
> b. the discovery of his tomb and history's view of him
> c. Qin's early years

After a short introduction, the article about Qin Shi Huangdi begins with _____, goes on to explain _____, and ends with _____.

2. Reread paragraph 2 in the article. Below, write a summary of the paragraph in no more than 25 words.

_____

_____

_____

_____

Reread your summary and decide whether it covers the important ideas in the paragraph. Next, decide how to shorten the summary to 15 words or less without leaving out any essential information. Write this summary below.

_____

_____

3. Choose the best one-sentence paraphrase for the following sentence from the article:

"Carved in a special clay called terracotta, the 8,000 soldiers were full-size adults, each about six feet tall."

☐ a. Each of 8,000 soldiers carved a six-foot statue in a special clay called terra cotta.

☐ b. The 8,000 statues of soldiers were carved from terra cotta clay, and each full-size soldier was about six feet tall.

☐ c. About 8,000 soldiers who were at least six feet tall were turned to terra cotta clay.

> _____ Number of correct answers
>
> Record your personal assessment of your work on the Critical Thinking Chart on page 136.

Critical Thinking

Put an X in the box next to the correct answer for question 1. Follow the directions provided for the other questions.

1. Judging by the events in the article, you can predict that the following will happen next:

☐ a. Experts will decide that the tomb is not worth saving.

☐ b. Experts will continue to search for more objects near Qin's tomb.

☐ c. People will allow the tomb to be hidden again.

2. Choose from the letters below to correctly complete the following statement. Write the letters on the lines.

   In the article, _____ and _____ are alike in the way that they planned for the afterlife.

   a. Qin's regent

   b. Egyptian pharaohs

   c. Qin Shi Huangdi

3. Think about cause-effect relationships in the article. Fill in the blanks in the cause-effect chart, drawing from the letters below.

Cause	Effect
Qin was too young to rule.	_____
A violent storm blew up when Qin was hiking.	_____
_____	The clay soldiers all face east.

   a. Qin feared attacks from eastern enemies.

   b. A regent ruled until Qin was 21.

   c. Qin had workers cut down trees.

4. Which paragraphs from the article provide evidence that supports your answer to question 3?

   _____

   _____ Number of correct answers

   Record your personal assessment of your work on the Critical Thinking Chart on page 136.

Personal Response

Would you recommend this article to other students? Explain.

_____

_____

_____

_____

Self-Assessment

I was confused on question # _____ in section _____ because

_____

_____

_____

_____

CRITICAL THINKING

THE INVENTING OF LIQUID PAPER

As soon as Bette Nesmith tried out her new IBM electric typewriter, she knew she was in trouble. The machine was much too fast and sensitive for her. Bette, a secretary at a bank in Dallas, Texas, had always gotten by with her old manual typewriter. It had no power. Its keys had to be pushed down hard to strike the paper. The slow machine was just fine for a slow typist. Also, the ink on the old ribbons was easy to deal with—Bette could easily erase all her mistakes with a pencil eraser.

2   Her new typewriter, though, was a nightmare. The keys would strike with the slightest touch. The machine used a special carbon-film ribbon. Although this made clearer letters, it also caused the ink to smudge easily. Bette couldn't erase her mistakes without making an ugly mess on the paper. With her old machine, Bette had been able to hide the fact that she didn't type very well. The IBM made it hard for her to do that anymore.

3   Bette was a divorced mother trying to support her young son, Michael. She didn't want to lose her job just because she was a poor typist. So she struggled along as best she could, constantly

Bette Nesmith made life easier for typists around the world with her invention of Liquid Paper.

frazzled by the challenges of this new typewriter.

4   Then, in 1954, Bette helped design holiday windows at the bank to earn a little extra money. She noticed that the people painting the window designs didn't erase their mistakes. They just painted over them. That gave her a simple—but brilliant—idea. She thought, why not paint over *my typing mistakes?*

5   Bette Nesmith went home that evening and mixed up some white tempera paint in a bottle. She also found an old watercolor brush. (Bette had wanted to be an artist, but the divorce had forced her to become a secretary instead.) The following day—presto!—all her typing errors disappeared. There was no fuss, no mess. From then on, whenever Bette made a mistake, she simply painted over it. Bette didn't feel quite right about what she was doing. To her, it seemed like she was cheating. People in her office believed she had become a perfect typist when, in fact, she was still quite marginal. Still, her secret enabled her to turn out typed papers faster and neater than ever.

6   In time, other secretaries at the bank found out about Bette's white paint. They, too, made mistakes and wanted their own bottles. By 1956, Bette was bottling her paint and selling it. She even put on her own label marked "Mistake Out."

7   Bette didn't have enough money to produce her little bottles in a big way. Still, she worked to make her paint better. She couldn't afford to hire a chemist. So she read all the chemical books she could and blended different mixtures in an old-fashioned mixer. She also had help from a high school chemistry teacher and a local paint company. At last, she came up with a formula for a paint that was both quick-drying and barely detectable. Bette soon changed the name of her product. She called it "Liquid Paper."

8   Bette took her paint to IBM. If anyone would buy her idea, she thought, it would be the maker of electric typewriters. But IBM wasn't interested in marketing her Liquid Paper. They told her to improve her product even more and come back again later.

Liquid Paper is now marketed by The Gillette Company and is available in several different shades to match the various paper colors used in offices.

9　　Bette had other thoughts. Instead of going back to IBM, she stayed home. With the help of her son Michael and some of his friends, she bottled the paint in her kitchen and garage on weekends. The crew squeezed Liquid Paper from old ketchup containers into little bottles. By 1957, Bette had applied for a patent and a trademark. She was selling about 100 bottles a month.

10　　Then, in 1958, Bette got her big break. Liquid Paper got a brief but favorable notice in an office supply magazine. It was named one of the magazine's "top 50 new products of the month." Over 500 orders flooded in from around the country. General Electric alone ordered more than 400 bottles in three colors. Bette left her job at the bank. Producing Liquid Paper became her full-time job. She focused all her energy on making and marketing this new product.

11　　In its early years, Bette's operation lost money. But Bette never lost faith in her idea. By 1964, she had boosted production to 5,000 bottles a week and was finally making money. Four years later, the company was selling a million bottles a year.

12　　By 1975, Bette built a huge new plant. She could turn out 25 million bottles of Liquid Paper a year. Her company employed 200 people. And Liquid Paper was sold around the world.

13　　Clearly, IBM had make a mistake. The company should have had as much faith in Liquid Paper as Bette Nesmith had. In 1979, Bette sold her company to The Gillette Company for nearly $48 million. That's not bad for a single idea and an unshakable faith in it. Bette died in 1980. She left half her money to charity and gave the other half to her son, Michael.

14　　By then, Michael Nesmith was a household name. He had been a guitar player for the famous made-for-TV band known as "The Monkees." Like his mother, Michael had one great idea. He was the first person ever to create a TV show based on music videos. It was this idea that inspired Time-Warner to create the successful television station called MTV. 🍃

If you have been timed while reading this article, enter your reading time below. Then turn to the Words-per-Minute Table on page 133 and look up your reading speed (words per minute). Enter your reading speed on the graph on page 134.

Reading Time: Lesson 9

_____ : _____
Minutes　　*Seconds*

A Finding the Main Idea

One statement below expresses the main idea of the article. One statement is too general, or too broad. The other statement explains only part of the article; it is too narrow. Label the statements using the following key:

M—Main Idea   **B—Too Broad**   **N—Too Narrow**

_____ 1. Secretary Bette Nesmith invented Liquid Paper, a way to correct typing mistakes.

_____ 2. Useful inventions often come from unexpected sources.

_____ 3. Bette Nesmith tried to sell her invention to IBM, a maker of electric typewriters.

_____ Score 15 points for a correct M answer.

_____ Score 5 points for each correct B or N answer.

_____ **Total Score:** Finding the Main Idea

B Recalling Facts

How well do you remember the facts in the article? Put an X in the box next to the answer that correctly completes each statement about the article.

1. One reason Bette Nesmith didn't like her electric typewriter was that
   ☐ a. it used a ribbon that made erasing messy.
   ☐ b. it was slow.
   ☐ c. its keys had to be pushed really hard.

2. Bette Nesmith first got the idea for Liquid Paper when she
   ☐ a. made her first typing mistake.
   ☐ b. was painting a portrait.
   ☐ c. was working on a holiday window.

3. By 1957, Nesmith was selling
   ☐ a. over one million bottles of Liquid Paper per year.
   ☐ b. about 5,000 bottles per year.
   ☐ c. about 1,200 bottles per year.

4. Nesmith sold her company to The Gillette Company for
   ☐ a. $1 million.
   ☐ b. $48 million.
   ☐ c. $100 million.

5. Bette Nesmith's son, Michael, was part of the rock group
   ☐ a. The Monkees.
   ☐ b. The Beatles.
   ☐ c. The Tigers.

Score 5 points for each correct answer.

_____ **Total Score:** Recalling Facts

C Making Inferences

When you combine your own experience and information from a text to draw a conclusion that is not directly stated in that text, you are making an inference. Below are five statements that may or may not be inferences based on information in the article. Label the statements using the following key:

C—Correct Inference   **F—Faulty Inference**

_____ 1. Bette Nesmith was not the only typist who needed a way to get rid of mistakes.

_____ 2. Most secretaries earn a steady income; many artists do not.

_____ 3. Secretaries are all excellent typists.

_____ 4. All successful companies earn a profit during their first year.

_____ 5. Artists are less likely to make mistakes than secretaries are.

Score 5 points for each correct answer.

_____ **Total Score:** Making Inferences

D Using Words Precisely

Each numbered sentence below contains an underlined word or phrase from the article. Following the sentence are three definitions. One definition is closest to the meaning of the underlined word. One definition is opposite or nearly opposite. Label those two definitions using the following key. Do not label the remaining definition.

C—Closest   **O—Opposite or Nearly Opposite**

1. The machine was much too fast and <u>sensitive</u> for her.

    _____ a. complicated

    _____ b. quick to react

    _____ c. deadened

2. Bette, a secretary at a bank in Dallas, Texas, had always gotten by with her old <u>manual</u> typewriter.

    _____ a. done by hand

    _____ b. automatic

    _____ c. fancy

3. So she struggled along as best she could, constantly <u>frazzled</u> by the challenges of this new typewriter.

    _____ a. refreshed

    _____ b. surprised

    _____ c. exhausted

4. People in her office believed she had become a perfect typist when, in fact, she was still quite <u>marginal</u>.

    _____ a. excellent

    _____ b. barely adequate

    _____ c. nervous

5. Liquid Paper got a brief but <u>favorable</u> notice in an office supply magazine.

_____ a. critical and disapproving

_____ b. interesting

_____ c. complimentary

_____ Score 3 points for each correct C answer.

_____ Score 2 points for each correct O answer.

_____ **Total Score:** Using Words Precisely

Enter the four total scores in the spaces below, and add them together to find your Reading Comprehension Score. Then record your score on the graph on page 135.

Score	Question Type	Lesson 9
_____	Finding the Main Idea	
_____	Recalling Facts	
_____	Making Inferences	
_____	Using Words Precisely	
_____	**Reading Comprehension Score**	

Author's Approach

Put an X in the box next to the correct answer.

1. What is the author's purpose in writing "The Inventing of Liquid Paper"?
   - ☐ a. To encourage the reader to invent something
   - ☐ b. To inform the reader about a creative woman who followed through on a good idea
   - ☐ c. To emphasize the differences between manual and electric typewriters

2. From the statements below, choose those that you believe the author would agree with.
   - ☐ a. Bette Nesmith's invention was a success because it was useful to so many people.
   - ☐ b. It took courage for Bette Nesmith to leave her full-time job and devote her time to her new invention.
   - ☐ c. Bette Nesmith should have sold the idea for her invention to IBM instead of bothering to produce Liquid Paper herself.

3. How is the author's purpose for writing the article expressed in paragraph 13?
   - ☐ a. The author points out that Nesmith left half her money to charity.
   - ☐ b. The author points out that Nesmith had faith in her good idea.
   - ☐ c. The author points out that IBM made a mistake.

4. The author tells this story mainly by
   - ☐ a. describing events in the order they happened.
   - ☐ b. comparing different topics.
   - ☐ c. telling different stories about the same topic.

_____ Number of correct answers

Record your personal assessment of your work on the Critical Thinking Chart on page 136.

Summarizing and Paraphrasing

Follow the directions provided for question 1. Put an X in the box next to the correct answer for question 2.

1. Look for the important ideas and events in paragraphs 8 and 9. Summarize those paragraphs in one or two sentences.

_____

_____

_____

2. Below are summaries of the article. Choose the summary that says all the most important things about the article but in the fewest words.

☐ a. Bette Nesmith had wanted to be an artist, but she took a job as a secretary. Later she invented a useful product and produced and sold her invention full-time.

☐ b. Bette Nesmith, a secretary at a bank, hated her IBM electric typewriter because it made it so hard to erase typing errors. For that reason, she went to work trying to come up with a way to cover up her typing mistakes. After she did some chemistry research, she invented a product she called Liquid Paper.

☐ c. Secretary Bette Nesmith invented Liquid Paper, a way to cover up typing mistakes. She worked hard to produce and sell her invention. Her hard work paid off when she sold her company for $48 million.

_____ Number of correct answers

Record your personal assessment of your work on the Critical Thinking Chart on page 136.

Record your personal assessment of your work on the Critical Thinking Chart on page 136.

Critical Thinking

Put an X in the box next to the correct answer.

1. Which of the following statements from the article is an opinion rather than a fact?

☐ a. "In its early years, Bette's operation lost money."

☐ b. "That's not bad for a single idea and an unshakable faith in it."

☐ c. "She noticed that the people painting the window designs didn't erase their mistakes."

2. What was the effect of Bette Nesmith's frustration with the difficulty of erasing typing errors?

☐ a. She got a divorce.

☐ b. She became a secretary to support herself and her son.

☐ c. She invented Liquid Paper to cover up mistakes.

3. Of the following theme categories, which ones would this story fit into?

☐ a. Trust yourself.

☐ b. Don't rock the boat.

☐ c. Necessity is the mother of invention.

4. If you were an inventor, how could you use the information in the article to present your product to the buying public?

☐ a. Like Bette Nesmith, quit your job.

☐ b. Like Bette Nesmith, first try to sell your idea to IBM.

☐ c. Like Bette Nesmith, make your product by yourself at first.

5. What did you have to do to answer question 4?

☐ a.   find an opinion (what someone thinks about something)

☐ b.   find a description (how something looks)

☐ c.   draw a conclusion (a sensible statement based on the text and
         your experience)

_____ Number of correct answers

Record your personal assessment of your work on the Critical
Thinking Chart on page 136.

I can't really understand how

_____

_____

_____

_____

Personal Response

Why do you think Bette Nesmith decided to work on her invention by
herself after IBM turned her offer down?

_____

_____

_____

_____

MACHU PICCHU
City in the Clouds

Machu Picchu lies hidden in the mountains of Peru. While it is not the Lost City of the Incas, it is still a fascinating place.

Hiram Bingham stood in the hot sun, squinting at a small wooden hut high in the mountains of Peru. He walked up to the Quechua Indian who stood outside the hut and began speaking to the man. In broken Spanish, Bingham asked the question he had been asking everyone he met. Did the man know anything about the Lost City of the Incas?

2 The Lost City of the Incas was a legendary place. People had whispered about it for centuries. It was said to be magnificent, a place filled with great temples and precious metals. Rumor had it that the lost city was hidden somewhere in these tangled jungles of Peru. But no one knew exactly where. There were hundreds of miles of dense wilderness to conceal it. Chances were good that no outsider would ever find it.

3 Still, Bingham was determined to try. A professor from Yale University, Bingham was enthralled by the story of the lost city. When the Spanish had arrived in Peru in the 1530s, they had quickly taken over the Inca capital of Cuzco. The leader of the Incas had fled into the mountains with his followers. Somewhere on a

remote mountainside, it was said, he and his three sons had set up another city, filled with the silver and gold they had brought with them. From there they supposedly ruled over their dynasty for 35 more years. And what a dynasty it was! Although they had no iron tools, the Incas were superb craftsmen. Despite their lack of a written language, they were fine architects and astronomers. And even without the wheel, they had found ways to transport goods along the thousands of miles of roads they had built.

4   Bingham didn't know if the story of the lost city was true. Many fortune hunters had looked for it without success. Even if such a city had existed, Bingham didn't know if there was any remnant of it left. But like all good explorers, he was willing to go to great lengths to find out. And so in 1911, Bingham brought a group of six men to Peru. Together they headed up into the mountains, hoping to succeed where others had failed.

5   For three weeks Bingham's group had tromped higher and higher into the jungle. Along the way, Bingham had talked to every native resident he found. Some had described ruins that sounded like the lost city. Encouraged, Bingham pushed on. Now, on July 23, he heard the Quechua Indian describe spectacular ruins just a few miles away. The ruins, said the Indian,

were called "Machu Picchu," or "old peak."

6   That night, Bingham made plans to hike to Machu Picchu. But by the next morning, rain had moved in. For hours Bingham waited for a break in the clouds. At last, at 10:07 A.M., the sky lightened and Bingham set out. A military escort went with him. The two men were guided by a local resident named Melchor Arteaga. Bingham had agreed to pay Arteaga one silver dollar in exchange for his services.

7   For the first two miles, the men stuck to a narrow trail. They trudged past palm trees, ducked under vines, and stepped over deadly snakes. They also passed beautiful orchids and brightly colored butterflies. At last, they reached a rushing river that cut through a deep canyon.

8   The only way to cross the water was over a makeshift bridge. The bridge was just a crude bundle of long, thin logs that someone had lashed together and laid across the water. Most travelers would have turned back at that point. But not Bingham. Determined to get across, he got on his hands and knees and crawled across the rickety structure.

9   An hour and a half later, the men reached a clearing where another Indian family lived in a tiny hut. Here Bingham's guide stopped, telling Bingham that the

family's eight-year-old boy would lead him the rest of the way.

10   And so Bingham followed the young boy down a faint jungle trail. As they rounded a bend, Bingham suddenly stepped into a clearing. He found himself

Hiram Bingham, who discovered Machu Picchu

standing in front of a series of terraces, with steps leading to many levels above and below him. Perfectly cut stone walls lined a path that led through these terraces. As Bingham walked along the path, he passed an enormous cave. It, too, was marked with finely cut stones.

11 Who was responsible for the intricate stonework? Bingham had little time to ponder this question, for the boy kept leading him onward. Soon they came to a long stairway. The boy told him to climb it. At the top, he said, there was much more to see.

12 Eagerly Bingham climbed the stairway. At the top, he could barely believe his eyes. He found himself at the edge of a huge plaza. All around him were the massive ruins of an ancient city. Stone streets wound in and out of sight. The roofs of buildings had worn away, but the sides of the dwellings were still intact. Bingham could see that the buildings had been constructed with great attention to detail. He noticed gracefully curving walls, beautifully shaped windows, and elaborate fountains. There was a huge temple. There were several palaces. And there were many workshops, bathhouses, storehouses, and private homes.

13 Bingham called the place "a wonderful old Inca city." He described it as "far more wonderful and interesting than [other Inca ruins.]" In fact, he said, "It fairly took

my breath away." Bingham doubted that Machu Picchu was the Lost City of the Incas. After all, he found no gold or silver anywhere on the premises. And the large number of temples made it look as though the place was a religious, rather than political, center.

14 As it turns out, Bingham's instincts were correct. Machu Picchu was not the lost capital of the Incas. Recently discovered clues show that the Lost City lay in a different part of Peru. No one has ever found it. Machu Picchu, it seems, was a different city, perhaps one devoted to the gods. Still, Bingham realized that it would have tremendous appeal to the outside world. He knew that seeing Machu Picchu would give modern people a better understanding of the building skills, artistry, and culture of the ancient Incas.

15 Over the next several years, Bingham spread the word about his discovery. Eventually, tourists began coming to see Machu Picchu for themselves. What they saw was vivid proof of just how talented the Incas were. The stonework in the city was amazing. Many of the stones had six or more sides. They had been cut and polished to exact dimensions. Then they had been fitted together so perfectly that the blade of a knife could not slip between them.

16 How the Incas managed to do this was—and still is—a mystery. Many of the

stones weighed several tons each. The Incas had no work animals to drag the stones from nearby quarries. How did they move the massive blocks? They had no iron tools. How did they carve the hard stones so precisely?

17 Because of these mysteries, some people have suggested that Machu Picchu was built by aliens from another planet. But the truth is simpler than that. The Incas obviously knew many secrets of art and architecture. Over the years, they sharpened their skills and perfected their crafts. It is a pity that such an advanced society was wiped out by invaders. But it is a blessing that they left behind Machu Picchu as a silent testimony to all they had learned. 🍃

If you have been timed while reading this article, enter your reading time below. Then turn to the Words-per-Minute Table on page 133 and look up your reading speed (words per minute). Enter your reading speed on the graph on page 134.

Reading Time: Lesson 10

_____ : _____

Minutes   Seconds

A Finding the Main Idea

One statement below expresses the main idea of the article. One statement is too general, or too broad. The other statement explains only part of the article; it is too narrow. Label the statements using the following key:

M—Main Idea   **B—Too Broad**   **N—Too Narrow**

_____ 1. It is exciting to find a treasure that has been "lost" for centuries.

_____ 2. Machu Picchu turned out not to be the Lost City of the Incas that Hiram Bingham had been searching for.

_____ 3. In 1911, Hiram Bingham was led to an ancient Inca city known to only local residents; he spread word of his discovery to the rest of the world.

_____ Score 15 points for a correct M answer.

_____ Score 5 points for each correct B or N answer.

_____ **Total Score:** Finding the Main Idea

B Recalling Facts

How well do you remember the facts in the article? Put an X in the box next to the answer that correctly completes each statement about the article.

1. Hiram Bingham was a professor from
   - ☐ a. Oberlin College.
   - ☐ b. Stanford University.
   - ☐ c. Yale University.

2. According to legend, the Lost City of the Incas was built around
   - ☐ a. 250 B.C.
   - ☐ b. 1530.
   - ☐ c. 1911

3. Bingham found Machu Picchu
   - ☐ a. by the Amazon River.
   - ☐ b. in the jungles of Mexico.
   - ☐ c. in the mountains of Peru.

4. Machu Picchu looks like it was a
   - ☐ a. religious center.
   - ☐ b. political center.
   - ☐ c. center of trade.

5. According to the article, one of the mysteries of Machu Picchu is how the Incas
   - ☐ a. grew enough food to feed all the citizens.
   - ☐ b. communicated with people in other cities.
   - ☐ c. moved massive stone blocks to make the city.

Score 5 points for each correct answer.

_____ **Total Score:** Recalling Facts

C | Making Inferences

When you combine your own experience and information from a text to draw a conclusion that is not directly stated in that text, you are making an inference. Below are five statements that may or may not be inferences based on information in the article. Label the statements using the following key:

C—Correct Inference   **F—Faulty Inference**

_____ 1. Hiram Bingham was bitterly disappointed that he never found the Lost City of the Incas.

_____ 2. The Incas were as skilled at building cities as the Spanish were.

_____ 3. Hiram Bingham was expert at speaking both Spanish and Indian languages.

_____ 4. Bingham could probably have found Machu Picchu even without any help from local residents.

_____ 5. Many hundreds or even thousands of people must have lived in Machu Picchu.

Score 5 points for each correct answer.

_____ **Total Score:** Making Inferences

D | Using Words Precisely

Each numbered sentence below contains an underlined word or phrase from the article. Following the sentence are three definitions. One definition is closest to the meaning of the underlined word. One definition is opposite or nearly opposite. Label those two definitions using the following key. Do not label the remaining definition.

C—Closest   **O—Opposite or Nearly Opposite**

1. A professor from Yale University, Bingham was <u>enthralled by</u> the story of the lost city.

_____ a. fascinated by

_____ b. indifferent to

_____ c. frightened by

2. The only way to cross the water was over a <u>makeshift</u> bridge.

_____ a. permanent

_____ b. temporary

_____ c. swaying

3. Determined to get across, he got on his hands and knees and crawled across the <u>rickety</u> structure.

_____ a. shaky

_____ b. wooden

_____ c. stable and firm

4. Who was responsible for the <u>intricate</u> stonework?

_____ a. simple

_____ b. complicated

_____ c. beautiful

5. The roofs of buildings had worn away, but the sides of the dwellings were still <u>intact</u>.

_____ a. visible

_____ b. in pieces

_____ c. complete and undamaged

_____ Score 3 points for each correct C answer.

_____ Score 2 points for each correct O answer.

_____ **Total Score:** Using Words Precisely

Enter the four total scores in the spaces below, and add them together to find your Reading Comprehension Score. Then record your score on the graph on page 135.

Score	Question Type	Lesson 10
_____	Finding the Main Idea	
_____	Recalling Facts	
_____	Making Inferences	
_____	Using Words Precisely	
_____	**Reading Comprehension Score**	

Author's Approach

Put an X in the box next to the correct answer.

1. The author uses the first sentence of the article to
   - ☐ a. inform the reader about the setting of the article.
   - ☐ b. describe the mountains of Peru.
   - ☐ c. entertain the reader with a pleasant story about Peru.

2. What does the author mean by the statement "The Lost City of the Incas was a legendary place"?
   - ☐ a. The Lost City of the Incas was an enormous place.
   - ☐ b. The Lost City was especially important to the Incas.
   - ☐ c. Many stories were told about the Lost City of the Incas, but no one knew if it was a real place.

3. Which of the following statements from the article best describes Machu Picchu?
   - ☐ a. "It was said to be magnificent, a place filled with great temples and precious metals."
   - ☐ b. "No one has ever found it."
   - ☐ c. "And the large number of temples made it look as though the place was a religious, rather than political, center."

4. Judging by statements from the article "Machu Picchu: City in the Clouds," you can conclude that the author wants the reader to think that
   - ☐ a. Machu Picchu would be a wonderful sight to see.
   - ☐ b. Machu Picchu is pretty much like any other city.
   - ☐ c. Machu Picchu was probably built by aliens from outer space.

_____ Number of correct answers

Record your personal assessment of your work on the Critical Thinking Chart on page 136.

CRITICAL THINKING

Summarizing and Paraphrasing

Follow the directions provided for question 1. Put an X in the box next to the correct answer for question 2.

1. Complete the following one-sentence summary of the article using the lettered phrases from the phrase bank below. Write the letters on the lines.

> **Phrase Bank:**
> a. Bingham's efforts to find the Lost City of the Incas
> b. a discussion about lost secrets of the Incas
> c. how Bingham found and spread the news about Machu Picchu

The article about Hiram Bingham and Machu Picchu begins with _____, goes on to explain _____, and ends with _____.

2. Read the statement about the article below. Then read the paraphrase of that statement. Choose the reason that best tells why the paraphrase does not say the same thing as the statement.

Statement: Bingham found himself standing by many terraces, with steps leading to levels above him and below him.

Paraphrase: Bingham saw that there were steps leading down to many terraces below him.

☐ a. Paraphrase says too much.
☐ b. Paraphrase doesn't say enough.
☐ c. Paraphrase doesn't agree with the statement about the article.

> _____ Number of correct answers
>
> Record your personal assessment of your work on the Critical Thinking Chart on page 136.

Critical Thinking

Follow the directions provided for question 1. Put an X in the box next to the correct answer for the other questions.

1. For each statement below, write O if it expresses an opinion or write F if it expresses a fact.

_____ a. It would be more exciting to find the Lost City of the Incas than to find Machu Picchu.

_____ b. Machu Picchu should have been left alone, protected from curious tourists.

_____ c. When the Spanish arrived in Peru, they took over the Inca capital, Cuzco.

2. Considering Hiram Bingham's actions as described in this article, you can predict that he would

☐ a. continue to search for the Lost City of the Incas.
☐ b. try to make a great deal of money through his discovery.
☐ c. destroy Machu Picchu.

3. How is Hiram Bingham's experience related to the theme of this book?

☐ a. He faced difficulties and dangers in Peru.
☐ b. He searched for the Lost City of the Incas.
☐ c. He found a city that many people did not know existed.

4. If you were an explorer looking for a lost city, how could you use the information in the article to find the city?

☐ a. Like Hiram Bingham, look near Machu Picchu.
☐ b. Like Hiram Bingham, ask for help from local residents.
☐ c. Like Hiram Bingham, become a professor at Yale.

5. What did you have to do to answer question 1?

☐ a. find an opinion (what someone thinks about something)

☐ b. find a description (how something looks)

☐ c. find a reason (why something is the way it is)

_____ Number of correct answers

Record your personal assessment of your work on the Critical Thinking Chart on page 136.

Personal Response

If I were the author, I would change

_____

_____

_____

_____

because

_____

_____

_____

Self-Assessment

One of the things I did best when reading this article was

_____

_____

_____

_____

I believe I did this well because

_____

_____

_____

_____

CRITICAL THINKING

ONE MAN'S SEARCH FOR HIS ROOTS

Alex Haley leaned over the railing of the *African Star* and stared at the inviting sea below. Just one step, he thought, and it would all be over. "Simply step through this rail and drop into the sea, and I'd be out of my misery forever," he recalled thinking. Then there would be "no more debts, no more deadlines, no more agonizing over slavery, no more nothing."

2   But Haley didn't jump. He heard voices in his head telling him not to kill himself. The voices urged him to go on with his book. "I knew exactly who [the voices] were," he said. "They were Bell, Kizzy, Chicken George, Cousin Georgia, my grandma—all those ancestors of mine." Haley turned away from the railing. Back in his stateroom, he sat down and cried for hours.

3   That night Haley went down into the dark hold in the *African Star*, as he had done several times before. He went into the bowels of the ship to gain a sense of what his African ancestors had experienced after they had been taken as slaves. First, Haley stripped down to the waist. Then he lay down on a rough board

between bales of raw rubber and closed his eyes. In his own words, Haley tried to imagine what it was like "to lie there in chains, in filth, hearing the cries of…other men screaming, babbling, praying, and dying around you."

4   After four nights of this, Haley broke through whatever it was that had been holding him back. He knew he could finish his book. "I felt for the first time that I *was* [the slave] Kunta Kinte," said Haley. "From that moment on, I had no problem with writing what his senses had registered crossing the ocean."

5   To get to that point, Haley had traveled a grinding and torturous road. He had become a writer while serving for 20 years in the U.S. Coast Guard. After leaving the service in 1959, he devoted himself to freelance writing. It was a real struggle. He got hundreds of rejection slips. He had no money most of the time. Still, he turned down well-paying jobs in order to keep writing. After three years, his determination paid off. He sold some articles. He even began to write regularly for some major magazines such as the *Reader's Digest*.

6   Then, in 1965, Haley co-wrote *The Autobiography of Malcolm X*. The book was a huge success. It sold over six million copies and was published in eight languages. He could now call his own shots.

He could easily earn $100,000 a year by writing short articles and lecturing. No one would have faulted him if he had taken this easy path. But he had something else in mind. As an African American, Haley burned with a desire to find out about his family's history. He wanted to trace his roots all the way back to Africa.

7   Haley didn't have much to work with. He knew only a little about his ancestors and a few African words taught to him by

Author Alex Haley spent years researching Roots. *Here he is shown on the set of* Roots II, *the sequel to the original television movie.*

Slaves were kept in shackles and chains when they were transported from Africa, as shown in this scene from the miniseries Roots.

his grandmother. But these slender clues were enough to encourage him. He began checking libraries and census records. He also consulted a language expert to trace the words his grandmother had taught him. His quest soon became a consuming passion. He traveled more than half a million miles following clues and checking records.

8   In time, he traced his family tree back for eight generations. His search took him back to Juffure, an African village in the modern nation of Gambia. Here he found that he was a direct descendent of Kunta Kinte, a man who had been born in 1750 and sold into slavery 17 years later. When the villagers heard of Haley's identity, they embraced him as a long-lost son.

9   Despite this happy reunion, writing the book took an enormous personal toll on Haley. It drove him to the railing of the *African Star*. All the research and travel cost money. His publishers, Doubleday & Company and the *Reader's Digest*, had advanced him some cash. But that money was soon gone. Next, he borrowed from old friends. "I owed everybody I had been able to borrow from," he later said. "It was humiliating." In addition, his publishers pressed him to write faster. Haley missed

five deadlines. He had to keep asking for a little more time.

10   Worse, Haley was riddled with self-doubt. Was he up to the job of writing this book? After all, what did he really know about slavery? What he did he know about the pain and suffering of Africans who had been sold into slavery and shipped to America? "I asked myself," he once said, "what right had I to be sitting in a carpeted high-rise apartment writing about what it was like in the hold of a slave ship?" At other times, sheer rage over slavery itself stymied his writing. He said he felt "like going back through history swinging an axe at the society that permitted slavery to happen."

11   In the end, though, Haley overcame all these obstacles. After 12 grueling years, he at last finished the book. In 1976, Doubleday published it under the title *Roots: The Saga of an American Family*. *Roots* was an engrossing blend of fact and fiction. Haley called it "faction." The book was a runaway bestseller. It was translated into 30 languages and sold millions of copies. A year later, *Roots* was turned into an ABC TV miniseries. It shattered all ratings records at the time. More than 130 million people saw at least one episode of

the eight-part series. *Roots* changed the way many Americans—black and white—looked at themselves and their history.

12   Alex Haley died in 1992. But he never lost sight of the road he had traveled to find his roots. The royalties from the book and the TV show had made him a wealthy man. Still, in his mansion he hung a glass frame on the wall. In it, he placed two old sardine cans and 18 cents. These simple items reminded him that at one time this was all he had in the world. 🍂

If you have been timed while reading this article, enter your reading time below. Then turn to the Words-per-Minute Table on page 133 and look up your reading speed (words per minute). Enter your reading speed on the graph on page 134.

Reading Time: Lesson 11

_____ : _____
Minutes   Seconds

A Finding the Main Idea

One statement below expresses the main idea of the article. One statement is too general, or too broad. The other statement explains only part of the article; it is too narrow. Label the statements using the following key:

M—Main Idea   **B—Too Broad**   **N—Too Narrow**

_____ 1. Many people feel an intense desire to learn about their family's past.

_____ 2. Although it was difficult for him, Alex Haley wrote a fascinating book about his family called *Roots*.

_____ 3. At one point while he was writing his book *Roots*, Alex Haley fell deeply into debt and depression.

_____ Score 15 points for a correct M answer.

_____ Score 5 points for each correct B or N answer.

_____ **Total Score:** Finding the Main Idea

B Recalling Facts

How well do you remember the facts in the article? Put an X in the box next to the answer that correctly completes each statement about the article.

1. Alex Haley devoted himself entirely to writing after 20 years in the U.S.
   - ☐ a. Navy.
   - ☐ b. Coast Guard.
   - ☐ c. Army.

2. Haley's first successful book was
   - ☐ a. *The Autobiography of Malcolm X*.
   - ☐ b. *Roots*.
   - ☐ c. *African Star*.

3. Haley discovered that one of his ancestors had lived in what is now the nation of
   - ☐ a. Kenya.
   - ☐ b. Tanzania.
   - ☐ c. Gambia.

4. When Haley returned to the village of his ancestor, the residents
   - ☐ a. embraced him as a long-lost son.
   - ☐ b. ignored him.
   - ☐ c. disliked him because he was a stranger.

5. Writing *Roots* took Alex Haley
   - ☐ a. five years.
   - ☐ b. 12 years.
   - ☐ c. 20 years.

Score 5 points for each correct answer.

_____ **Total Score:** Recalling Facts

C | Making Inferences

When you combine your own experience and information from a text to draw a conclusion that is not directly stated in that text, you are making an inference. Below are five statements that may or may not be inferences based on information in the article. Label the statements using the following key:

C—Correct Inference   F—Faulty Inference

_____ 1. Haley's publishers had great faith in his writing ability even before he completed *Roots*.

_____ 2. Haley's friends tried to talk him out of searching for his family's roots.

_____ 3. To be a writer, you need to be able to accept rejection.

_____ 4. It is difficult for many African Americans to find out much about their family histories.

_____ 5. Alex Haley was more interested in earning a good income than in learning about and sharing his family history.

Score 5 points for each correct answer.

_____ **Total Score:** Making Inferences

D | Using Words Precisely

Each numbered sentence below contains an underlined word or phrase from the article. Following the sentence are three definitions. One definition is closest to the meaning of the underlined word. One definition is opposite or nearly opposite. Label those two definitions using the following key. Do not label the remaining definition.

C—Closest   O—Opposite or Nearly Opposite

1. Then there would be "no more debts, no more deadlines, no more agonizing over slavery, no more nothing."

_____ a. rejoicing

_____ b. looking

_____ c. suffering

2. But it had been a grinding and torturous road for Haley.

_____ a. comfortable

_____ b. painful and difficult

_____ c. long

3. "I owed everybody I had been able to borrow from," he later said. "It was humiliating."

_____ a. intended to build self-esteem

_____ b. unpleasant

_____ c. embarrassing

4. At other times, sheer rage over slavery itself stymied his writing.

_____ a. blocked

_____ b. made easier

_____ c. affected

5. *Roots* was an <u>engrossing</u> blend of fact and fiction.

_____ a. old-fashioned

_____ b. very interesting

_____ c. dull

_____ Score 3 points for each correct C answer.

_____ Score 2 points for each correct O answer.

_____ **Total Score:** Using Words Precisely

Enter the four total scores in the spaces below, and add them together to find your Reading Comprehension Score. Then record your score on the graph on page 135.

Score	Question Type	Lesson 11
_____	Finding the Main Idea	
_____	Recalling Facts	
_____	Making Inferences	
_____	Using Words Precisely	
_____	**Reading Comprehension Score**	

Author's Approach

Put an X in the box next to the correct answer.

1. The main purpose of the first paragraph is to

☐ a. encourage the reader to take a sea cruise.

☐ b. compare Alex Haley with other writers.

☐ c. describe Alex Haley's feelings.

2. From the statements below, choose those that you believe the author would agree with.

☐ a. *Roots* helped Americans understand each other better.

☐ b. Not every event in *Roots* was based on facts; some events were fictional.

☐ c. Although *Roots* was an exciting book, the TV miniseries was dull.

3. What does the author imply by saying "Alex Haley leaned over the railing of the *African Star* and stared at the inviting sea below. Just one step, he [Alex Haley] thought, and it would all be over"?

☐ a. The ship was close to land.

☐ b. Committing suicide seemed easy and appealing to Alex Haley.

☐ c. Alex Haley was always very careful when he stood near the edge of the ship.

_____ Number of correct answers

Record your personal assessment of your work on the Critical Thinking Chart on page 136.

CRITICAL THINKING

Summarizing and Paraphrasing

Follow the directions provided for question 1. Put an X in the box next to the correct answer for question 2.

1. Reread paragraph 3 in the article. Below, write a summary of the paragraph in no more than 25 words.

_____

_____

_____

_____

Reread your summary and decide whether it covers the important ideas in the paragraph. Next, decide how to shorten the summary to 15 words or less without leaving out any essential information. Write this summary below.

_____

_____

_____

2. Choose the sentence that correctly restates the following sentence from the article:

"Here he [Haley] found that he was a direct descendent of Kunta Kinte, a man who had been born in 1750 and sold into slavery 17 years later."

☐ a. Haley discovered that he was descended from Kunta Kinte, who was born in 1750 and had been enslaved at the age of 17.

☐ b. Kunta Kinte had been born in 1750, and Alex Haley was sold into slavery when he was 17 years old.

☐ c. Kunta Kinte's ancestor had been born in 1750, and Haley learned about him when he was 17 years old.

_____ Number of correct answers

Record your personal assessment of your work on the Critical Thinking Chart on page 136.

Critical Thinking

Follow the directions provided for questions 1, 2, 3, and 5. Put an X in the box next to the correct answer for question 4.

1. For each statement below, write O if it expresses an opinion or write F if it expresses a fact.

_____ a. *Roots* was published in 1976.

_____ b. Alex Haley co-wrote *The Autobiography of Malcolm X*.

_____ c. Alex Haley was the greatest writer of the 20th century.

2. Choose from the letters below to correctly complete the following statement. Write the letters on the lines.

On the positive side, _____, but on the negative side _____.

a. Alex Haley had great emotional and financial difficulties while writing *Roots*

b. *Roots* helped readers understand the heritage of African Americans better

c. *Roots* was published by Doubleday & Company.

3. Choose from the letters below to correctly complete the following statement. Write the letters on the lines.

According to the article, _____ caused Alex Haley to _____, and the effect was _____.

a. become enraged

b. the unfairness of slavery

c. he became frustrated in his writing

4. Of the following theme categories, which would this story fit into?

☐ a. Remember and learn from the past.

☐ b. It's best to forget the past.

☐ c. What you don't know can't hurt you.

5. In which paragraph did you find your information or details to answer question 3?

_____ Number of correct answers

Record your personal assessment of your work on the Critical Thinking Chart on page 136.

Personal Response

Describe a time when you felt discouraged and ready to give up, like Alex Haley felt at times while he was writing *Roots*.

Self-Assessment

Before reading this article, I already knew

CRITICAL THINKING

THE SECRET OF VACCINATION

A speckled monster was terrorizing Europe during the 18th century. Each year more than a million Europeans fell victim to this gruesome killer. Most of the victims were young children. The monster played no favorites; it attacked people of all classes. In the 1700s it snuffed out five European monarchs. The speckled monster's name was smallpox, or simply "the pox."

2 Almost everyone who lived long enough came down with some form of smallpox. It was a highly contagious disease, spread in a number of ways. It could infect its victims through the air or by direct human contact. It could linger on clothing or bed sheets and infect anyone who touched these items. The first signs of the disease were a high fever, muscle pain, and a headache. Soon red spots, or speckles, appeared on the face and limbs of the victims. Then the rash swelled up into watery blisters. If the blisters began to bleed, the victim quickly died. If they scabbed over, the victim would likely recover. While smallpox killed many people, it could also be incredibly cruel to those who lived through it. Most survivors were left with ugly pock marks on their face and other disfiguring scars all over their bodies. Also, the disease left many victims blind.

3 Smallpox wasn't a problem in Europe alone. It was a world-wide affliction with a very long track record. In 1157 B.C. smallpox killed the Pharaoh Ramses V of Egypt. It showed up in the Far East about 2,000 years ago. The pox reached Europe about 710 A.D. And in the 1500s, the Spanish conquistadors brought it to the western hemisphere, where it killed about 3.5 million Aztecs in just two years.

4 There was no cure for smallpox. Once a person contracted the disease, all he or she could do was pray. Doctors merely tried to slow down this killing machine. And they had some limited success. Doctors in China, India, and Turkey noticed that if an individual survived smallpox, he or she never got it a second time. Getting the disease, it seemed, gave survivors immunity for life.

5 Working from these facts, doctors tried giving people a mild dose of the disease on purpose. They extracted the liquid from smallpox blisters and injected it into the skin of healthy people. When this procedure resulted in a mild case of the pox, everyone cheered. The subjects then had a lifetime guarantee against future illness. Unfortunately, the treatment gave many people a fatal case of the disease.

6 European doctors used this treatment to cut down the odds of dying of smallpox from over 20% to about 1%. Still, the

Europeans brought smallpox to the New World. The Indians had no immunities to the disease, and entire Indian villages were wiped out by it. This woodcut depicts smallpox deaths among the Wampanoags in Massachusetts in the 1600s.

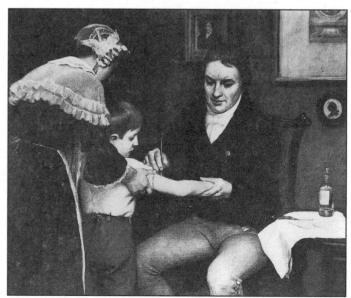

Dr. Edward Jenner performs the first smallpox vaccination on eight-year-old James Phipps in 1796.

practice was not as widely used as it might have been. The major problem was that smallpox, even in a mild form, was still highly contagious. So an inoculated individual could easily give the disease to others. He or she could become the source for a whole new outbreak of smallpox.

7   Edward Jenner, an English doctor, know all these facts about smallpox. He also knew there was one group who never seemed to suffer from the disease. These were people who worked closely with cows—particularly milkmaids. Milkmaids might come down with cowpox, a relatively harmless disease people got from cattle, but they somehow managed to avoid the deadly smallpox. From this fact, Jenner deduced that exposure to cowpox protected people against smallpox. Jenner began to wonder. What if he gave his patients a mild dose of cowpox as a way of vaccinating them against smallpox?

8   On May 14, 1796, Jenner tested his theory on an eight-year-old boy named James Phipps. James was the son of a laborer who often worked for Jenner. Jenner also enlisted the help of a milkmaid named Sarah Nelmes who had fresh cowpox blisters on her finger. Taking some of the clear fluid from Sarah's blisters, Jenner injected it into James. Then he waited. The boy soon developed a mild fever and a small blister—but nothing else. Six weeks later, on July 1, Jenner injected young James with smallpox. Happily, James didn't get the disease. Jenner was right: cowpox had protected James Phipps from smallpox.

9   Jenner's breakthrough was not accepted right away. After all, he had just one case to support his claim. In time, though, he successfully tested other people. Doctors in Europe and elsewhere began to use his cowpox vaccine. In 1801, Thomas Jefferson gave it to 200 of his neighbors. He also donated the vaccine to Native American tribes in Virginia.

10   Despite Jenner's vaccine, smallpox went on ravaging large parts of the world. There were two reasons for that. First, there was not enough cowpox vaccine for everyone. Cowpox occurred only in Europe and even there it was fairly rare. And second, there was no effective way to preserve the vaccine. It was easily compromised by heat. Spoiled vaccine, if used, often caused other diseases. So for well over 100 years after Jenner's work, smallpox went on rolling up its huge death toll. Even in Europe, there were occasional smallpox epidemics in the 19th century. One such outbreak killed about half a million people. In underdeveloped parts of the world, smallpox raged unchecked.

11   By the 1930s, however, a much better vaccine had been developed. The new vaccine did not spoil in heat. Also, it stayed pure and potent for a long time. And because it did not cost much to make, it became much more widely available. In 1967, the World Health Organization (WHO) began a worldwide campaign to abolish smallpox. Doctors and nurses gave the vaccine to children everywhere. The campaign was a huge success. In 1980, WHO announced that smallpox had been wiped out. Thanks to Edward Jenner and many others, the universal dread of smallpox is now a thing of the past.

If you have been timed while reading this article, enter your reading time below. Then turn to the Words-per-Minute Table on page 133 and look up your reading speed (words per minute). Enter your reading speed on the graph on page 134.

Reading Time: Lesson 12

_____ : _____
Minutes   Seconds

A | Finding the Main Idea

One statement below expresses the main idea of the article. One statement is too general, or too broad. The other statement explains only part of the article; it is too narrow. Label the statements using the following key:

M—Main Idea   **B—Too Broad**   **N—Too Narrow**

_____ 1. An English doctor named Edward Jenner searched for and found a way to prevent smallpox. His work led to a vaccine that wiped out the disease.

_____ 2. Smallpox was a terrible disease.

_____ 3. Edward Jenner tested his vaccine on an eight-year-old boy.

_____ Score 15 points for a correct M answer.

_____ Score 5 points for each correct B or N answer.

_____ **Total Score:** Finding the Main Idea

B | Recalling Facts

How well do you remember the facts in the article? Put an X in the box next to the answer that correctly completes each statement about the article.

1. The first signs of smallpox were
   ☐ a. nausea and vomiting.
   ☐ b. a high fever, muscle pain, and a headache.
   ☐ c. red spots that swelled to watery blisters.

2. Smallpox reached Europe around
   ☐ a. 1200 B.C.
   ☐ b. 1700.
   ☐ c. A.D. 710.

3. Edward Jenner was a doctor in
   ☐ a. the United States.
   ☐ b. Egypt.
   ☐ c. England.

4. Jenner noticed that smallpox didn't affect
   ☐ a. milkmaids.
   ☐ b. housemaids.
   ☐ c. children.

5. Jenner made his vaccine from
   ☐ a. chemicals in his laboratory.
   ☐ b. fluid from cowpox blisters.
   ☐ c. fluid from smallpox blisters.

Score 5 points for each correct answer.

_____ **Total Score:** Recalling Facts

C Making Inferences

When you combine your own experience and information from a text to draw a conclusion that is not directly stated in that text, you are making an inference. Below are five statements that may or may not be inferences based on information in the article. Label the statements using the following key:

C—Correct Inference   F—Faulty Inference

_____ 1. James Phipps, the boy on whom Jenner tested his vaccine, could have died in the experiment.

_____ 2. Edward Jenner became very rich as a result of his discovery of the smallpox vaccine.

_____ 3. Most people were especially kind to smallpox survivors with pock marks on their faces.

_____ 4. The Spanish conquistadors intentionally brought smallpox to the Americas.

_____ 5. Now that smallpox has been conquered, there are no diseases that strike fear all around the world.

Score 5 points for each correct answer.

_____ **Total Score:** Making Inferences

D Using Words Precisely

Each numbered sentence below contains an underlined word or phrase from the article. Following the sentence are three definitions. One definition is closest to the meaning of the underlined word. One definition is opposite or nearly opposite. Label those two definitions using the following key. Do not label the remaining definition.

C—Closest   O—Opposite or Nearly Opposite

1. It was a highly underlined contagious disease, spread in a number of ways.

_____ a. catching

_____ b. not able to be transmitted

_____ c. dangerous

2. Most survivors were left with ugly pock marks on their face and other disfiguring scars all over their bodies.

_____ a. beautiful

_____ b. puzzling

_____ c. ugly

3. Getting the disease, it seemed, gave survivors immunity for life.

_____ a. problems

_____ b. freedom from disease

_____ c. greater likelihood of becoming ill

4. It [the vaccine] was easily compromised by heat.

_____ a. evaporated

_____ b. maintained in a perfect state

_____ c. damaged

5. Thanks to Edward Jenner and many others, the <u>universal</u> dread of smallpox is now a thing of the past.

_____ a. limited

_____ b. widespread; affecting everyone

_____ c. terrible

_____ Score 3 points for each correct C answer.

_____ Score 2 points for each correct O answer.

_____ **Total Score:** Using Words Precisely

Enter the four total scores in the spaces below, and add them together to find your Reading Comprehension Score. Then record your score on the graph on page 135.

Score	Question Type	Lesson 12
_____	Finding the Main Idea	
_____	Recalling Facts	
_____	Making Inferences	
_____	Using Words Precisely	
_____	**Reading Comprehension Score**	

Author's Approach

Put an X in the box next to the correct answer.

1. The author uses the first paragraph of the article to
☐ a. inform the reader about life in 18th century Europe.
☐ b. emphasize the danger of smallpox.
☐ c. compare smallpox and chicken pox.

2. What does the author mean by the statement "Once a person contracted the disease, all he or she could do was pray"?
☐ a. People infected with smallpox could not live normal, active lives.
☐ b. Smallpox victims became very religious.
☐ c. There was no effective way of treating or curing smallpox.

3. What is the author's purpose in writing "The Secret of Vaccination"?
☐ a. To encourage the reader to take up research
☐ b. To inform the reader about how smallpox was conquered
☐ c. To convey a mood of terror

4. How is the author's purpose for writing the article expressed in paragraph 11?
☐ a. The author points out that through the work of many people, smallpox has been wiped out.
☐ b. The author points out that in the 1930s a new vaccine was developed.
☐ c. The author describes the new smallpox vaccine.

_____ Number of correct answers

Record your personal assessment of your work on the Critical Thinking Chart on page 136.

CRITICAL THINKING

Summarizing and Paraphrasing

Put an X in the box next to the correct answer.

1. Below are summaries of the article. Choose the summary that says all the most important things about the article but in the fewest words.

☐ a. The vaccine that Edward Jenner discovered has led to other, better vaccines to wipe out disease.

☐ b. People all over the world had feared smallpox for centuries. Then Dr. Edward Jenner discovered that injecting people with fluid from cowpox blisters protected them from the disease. Now smallpox is no longer a worldwide threat.

☐ c. Even though Edward Jenner discovered a vaccine that made people immune from smallpox, people continued to contract the disease. That's because the vaccine easily became damaged when it was exposed to heat.

2. Choose the best one-sentence paraphrase for the following sentence from the article:

"They [doctors] extracted the liquid from smallpox blisters and injected it into the skin of healthy people."

☐ a. Healthy people often asked doctors to withdraw fluid from the blisters of smallpox victims in an attempt to cure them.

☐ b. Doctors injected smallpox victims with a little fluid taken from smallpox blisters.

☐ c. Fluid was taken from smallpox blisters and injected into people who did not have smallpox.

_____ Number of correct answers

Record your personal assessment of your work on the Critical Thinking Chart on page 136.

Critical Thinking

Put an X in the box next to the correct answer for questions 1 and 4. Follow the directions provided for the other questions.

1. From the information in paragraph 11, you can predict that if today you come down with a high fever, muscle pain, and a headache, you should

☐ a. be confident that you do not have smallpox.

☐ b. be pretty sure that you are catching smallpox.

☐ c. not be concerned at all.

2. Choose from the letters below to correctly complete the following statement. Write the letters on the lines.

In the article, _____ and _____ are different in their level of fear about smallpox.

a. people of 18th century Europe

b. Aztecs after the Spanish set up colonies in the Americas

c. people of today

3. Choose from the letters below to correctly complete the following statement. Write the letters on the lines.

According to the article, _____ caused them to _____, and the effect was _____.

a. develop cowpox

b. they became immune to smallpox

c. injecting healthy people with cowpox blister fluid

4. How is Edward Jenner's work with smallpox related to the theme of *Eureka*?

☐ a. Jenner's work led him to the solution to an age-old problem.

☐ b. Jenner carried out his experiments by himself.

☐ c. Jenner's work required a great deal of intelligence and care to be successful.

_____ Number of correct answers

Record your personal assessment of your work on the Critical Thinking Chart on page 136.

Personal Response

If you could ask the author of the article one question, what would it be?

_____

_____

_____

Self-Assessment

Which concepts or ideas from the article were difficult to understand?

_____

_____

_____

_____

Which were easy to understand?

_____

_____

_____

_____

THE DEAD SEA SCROLLS

The Dead Sea Scrolls were found in caves in Jordan, a country in the Middle East.

One day in 1947, a shepherd boy was tending his flock. He noticed that one of his goats had wandered off into the hills near the Dead Sea in what is now the nation of Jordan. As the boy looked for his lost goat, he spotted something out of the corner of his eye. It was a small opening to a cave in the face of a rocky cliff. Idly, the boy tossed a stone into the cave. But instead of hearing the stone echo as it bounced off the walls of the cave, he heard the sound of something shattering. What could it be?

2   At first, the unexpected noise frightened the boy, and he ran away. Later, however, he gathered his courage and returned to the cave, this time bringing a friend along. Hoping that there might be buried treasure hidden in the cave, the two boys squeezed into the narrow opening between the rocks. Then they dropped to the floor of a cave that was about six feet wide and 26 feet long.

3   What the two boys saw disappointed them. Instead of glittering treasure chests, they saw only a few clay jars. The boys opened the lid on one and peered in at what looked like lumps folded up in linen. They loosened the linen and found

wrapped inside several scrolls made from sheep's leather. The scrolls ranged from three feet to 24 feet in length. The boys' discovery wasn't the gold and jewels they had hoped for. But it was a fabulous treasure anyway. Their find, which became known as the Dead Sea Scrolls, turned out to be fragments from the Old Testament of the Bible.

4   The boys must have sensed they had stumbled onto something valuable. Otherwise, they would have just tossed the smelly manuscripts away. Instead, they tried to sell the scrolls to an antique dealer in Bethlehem. He wasn't interested. In his judgment, the scrolls had no value. A short while later, however, the boys found a buyer who gave them a few dollars for the scrolls. The buyer, in turn, sold half of the scrolls to the Hebrew University and the other half to a Syrian monk named Samuel.

5   At first, even the experts could not agree on the significance of the discovery. One specialist agreed with the dealer in Bethlehem. He called the scrolls "worth-less." Another labeled the Dead Sea Scrolls a "hoax." But soon other experts began to speak up. Dr. William Albright, an American archaeologist, examined the scrolls. He said they were an "absolutely incredible find." Albright went on to declare that the Dead Sea Scrolls were "the greatest manuscript discovery of modern times."

6   It turned out that the skeptics were wrong and Albright was right. The Dead Sea Scrolls were more than 2,000 years old. A special carbon test dated them from about 200 B.C. to A.D. 68. In other words, the scrolls were ancient.

7   The scrolls opened a whole new world to Bible scholars. Before the discovery, the oldest known Bible dated back only 1,100 years to the Middle Ages. In addition, the scrolls were the first manuscripts ever found in that particular part of the Middle East.

8   The Dead Sea Scrolls touched off a wave of discovery. Eager searchers looked for more caves and more scrolls. By 1956, they had found 10 more caves. Each one was a marvelous discovery in itself. Cave 2, for example, contained fragments of five books from the Old Testament. Less than a mile away, in Cave 3, researchers found the Copper Scroll. (All the other scrolls had been written on either leather or papyrus.) The Copper Scroll told the locations of hidden treasures of gold, silver, and precious oils. Cave 4 produced the most spectacular find of all. It wasn't really a cave. Rather, it was a hollowed-out chamber. Researchers found thousands of bits and pieces from almost every book in the Old Testament. They also found texts that were not biblical. These included books on war, psalms, and rules of conduct.

The Dead Sea Scrolls offered some new insights into the Old Testament, but mostly they confirmed what was already written.

9   Most of the scrolls were written in Hebrew. Some, however, were written in Aramaic, the language Jesus spoke. And a few of the scrolls were written in Greek. Most likely, the authors came from the a sect of Jews known as the Essenes. They probably hid the scrolls in A.D. 68 to protect them from an invading Roman army. When the Roman legions finally arrived, they sacked the community where the Essenes lived, but they never found the scrolls hidden in caves and underground chambers.

10   Why were the Dead Sea Scrolls so important? Why are they today considered to be "priceless?" For one thing, some of the scrolls were written during the time Jesus walked the earth. They offer a unique view of what life was like 2,000 years ago. Also, the oldest existing Bible up to their discovery had been translated from the Greek. Jews and Christians had no Bible written in the language of the people who actually wrote the Bible. Scholars thought it was possible that the long-forgotten people who translated the Bible got some things wrong. If so, they reasoned, the scrolls could challenge the fundamental beliefs of Judaism and Christianity.

11   As it turned out, the Dead Sea Scrolls did not lead to major changes in the Christian and Jewish faiths. The scrolls did offer new facts and insights. Some books in the Old Testament, for example, had to be changed a bit. But for the most part, the scrolls confirmed what was in the existing Bible. Although Jesus was not mentioned in the scrolls, there was nothing in them to dispute Christian beliefs. As Dr. Frank M. Cross, Jr. said, "No Christian need stand in dread of these texts."

12   The scrolls have helped us all understand the world and its people from 2,000 years ago. They have allowed us to see that world directly for the first time. In that sense, the scrolls truly are a priceless window to the past. 🍃

If you have been timed while reading this article, enter your reading time below. Then turn to the Words-per-Minute Table on page 133 and look up your reading speed (words per minute). Enter your reading speed on the graph on page 134.

Reading Time: Lesson 13

_____ : _____

Minutes   Seconds

A | Finding the Main Idea

One statement below expresses the main idea of the article. One statement is too general, or too broad. The other statement explains only part of the article; it is too narrow. Label the statements using the following key:

M—Main Idea　　　**B—Too Broad**　　　**N—Too Narrow**

_____　1.　A shepherd boy is responsible for discovering an important piece of history.

_____　2.　Carbon dating proved that the Dead Sea Scrolls came from an era between 200 B.C. and A.D. 70.

_____　3.　Scrolls found in 1947 have shed light on ancient life and have allowed scholars to make the Bible more clear and complete.

_____　Score 15 points for a correct M answer.

_____　Score 5 points for each correct B or N answer.

_____　**Total Score:** Finding the Main Idea

B | Recalling Facts

How well do you remember the facts in the article? Put an X in the box next to the answer that correctly completes each statement about the article.

1. The shepherd boy was tending his flock in the country now called
   - ☐ a. Israel.
   - ☐ b. Jordan.
   - ☐ c. Egypt.

2. The scrolls were made from
   - ☐ a. heavy paper.
   - ☐ b. linen.
   - ☐ c. sheep's leather.

3. The scrolls had probably been hidden when the
   - ☐ a. Greeks invaded the area.
   - ☐ b. area was flooded.
   - ☐ c. Roman army invaded the area.

4. Before the scrolls were found, the oldest available Bible had been
   - ☐ a. translated from the Greek language.
   - ☐ b. impossible to read.
   - ☐ c. lost.

5. The Dead Sea Scrolls are important because they
   - ☐ a. paint a picture of life 2,000 years ago.
   - ☐ b. were stored in caves.
   - ☐ c. were wrapped in linen.

Score 5 points for each correct answer.

_____　**Total Score:** Recalling Facts

C Making Inferences

When you combine your own experience and information from a text to draw a conclusion that is not directly stated in that text, you are making an inference. Below are five statements that may or may not be inferences based on information in the article. Label the statements using the following key:

C—Correct Inference   F—Faulty Inference

_____ 1. The Dead Sea Scrolls could have remained undiscovered for centuries if the shepherd boy hadn't found them.

_____ 2. Antique dealers don't always know the true value of items they see.

_____ 3. When the Romans conquered nations, they were careful to respect the property of the people who lived there.

_____ 4. No one understands the Aramaic language anymore.

_____ 5. There are many caves in the Dead Sea area of Jordan.

Score 5 points for each correct answer.

_____ **Total Score:** Making Inferences

D Using Words Precisely

Each numbered sentence below contains an underlined word or phrase from the article. Following the sentence are three definitions. One definition is closest to the meaning of the underlined word. One definition is opposite or nearly opposite. Label those two definitions using the following key. Do not label the remaining definition.

C—Closest   O—Opposite or Nearly Opposite

1. When the Roman legions finally arrived, they <u>sacked</u> the community where the Essenes lived....

_____ a. moved into

_____ b. treated with care and respect

_____ c. robbed and ruined

2. They offer a <u>unique</u> view of what life was like 2,000 years ago.

_____ a. one-of-a-kind

_____ b. run-of-the-mill

_____ c. holy

3. But for the most part, the scrolls <u>confirmed</u> what was in the existing Bible.

_____ a. backed up

_____ b. examined

_____ c. caused doubt about

4. Although Jesus was not mentioned in the scrolls, there was nothing in them to <u>dispute</u> Christian beliefs.

_____ a. agree with

_____ b. know about

_____ c. quarrel with

5. In that sense, the scrolls truly are a <u>priceless</u> window to the past.

_____ a. believable

_____ b. worthless

_____ c. so valuable as to be beyond price

_____ Score 3 points for each correct C answer.

_____ Score 2 points for each correct O answer.

_____ **Total Score:** Using Words Precisely

Enter the four total scores in the spaces below, and add them together to find your Reading Comprehension Score. Then record your score on the graph on page 135.

Score	Question Type	Lesson 13
_____	Finding the Main Idea	
_____	Recalling Facts	
_____	Making Inferences	
_____	Using Words Precisely	
_____	**Reading Comprehension Score**	

Author's Approach

Put an X in the box next to the correct answer.

1. The main purpose of the first paragraph is to
   ☐ a. describe the area around the Dead Sea.
   ☐ b. make the reader curious about what was in the cave.
   ☐ c. show how difficult it is to be a shepherd.

2. Which of the following statements from the article best describes the appearance of the Dead Sea Scrolls?
   ☐ a. "The scrolls opened a whole new world to Bible scholars."
   ☐ b. "They [the scrolls] off a unique view of what life was like 2,000 years ago."
   ☐ c. "The scrolls ranged from three to 24 feet in length."

3. In this article, "The scrolls touched off a wave of discovery" means
   ☐ a. many people became upset by the discovery of the scrolls.
   ☐ b. the scrolls were the last ancient objects found near the Dead Sea.
   ☐ c. the finding of the scrolls inspired others to search for ancient objects.

4. How is the author's purpose for writing the article expressed in paragraph 12?
   ☐ a. In this paragraph, the author tells when the scrolls were made.
   ☐ b. In this paragraph, the author explains why the discovery of the scrolls was important.
   ☐ c. In this paragraph, the author estimates the price of the scrolls.

_____ Number of correct answers

Record your personal assessment of your work on the Critical Thinking Chart on page 136.

Summarizing and Paraphrasing

Follow the directions provided for the questions.

1. Complete the following one-sentence summary of the article using the lettered phrases from the phrase bank below. Write the letters on the lines.

Phrase Bank:
a. a statement about the scrolls' real value
b. how the scrolls were received by experts
c. the shepherd boy's discovery

The article about "Dead Sea Scrolls" begins with _____, goes on to explain _____, and ends with _____.

2. Reread paragraph 9 in the article. Below, write a summary of the paragraph in no more than 25 words.

_____

_____

_____

Reread your summary and decide whether it covers the important ideas in the paragraph. Next, decide how to shorten the summary to 15 words or less without leaving out any essential information. Write this summary below.

_____

_____

_____

_____ Number of correct answers

Record your personal assessment of your work on the Critical Thinking Chart on page 136.

Critical Thinking

Follow the directions provided for questions 1 and 5. Put an X in the box next to the correct answer for the other questions.

1. For each statement below, write O if it expresses an opinion or write F if it expresses a fact.

_____ a. The boys who found the scrolls had been hoping to find gold and jewels.

_____ b. The Essenes should not have hidden the scrolls in such an out-of-the-way place.

_____ c. The finding of the Dead Sea Scrolls is the most important discovery of the 20th century.

2. From what William Albright said, you can predict that when the scrolls were found to be genuine, he

☐ a. felt proud of his own judgment.

☐ b. didn't really care anymore.

☐ c. was embarrassed about what he had said previously.

3. What was the cause of the two boys' search of the cave?

☐ a. They were frightened.

☐ b. They wanted to find ancient scrolls.

☐ c. They thought the cave might hold treasure.

4. If you were a archaeologist and you found an object you thought was ancient, how could you use the information in the article to help you determine its age?

☐ a. Consult just one expert for his or her opinion.

☐ b. Ask an antique dealer how old the object is.

☐ c. Carbon date the object you found.

5. In which paragraph did you find your information or details to answer question 3?

_____

_____ Number of correct answers

Record your personal assessment of your work on the Critical Thinking Chart on page 136.

Personal Response

I agree with the author because

_____

_____

_____

_____

Self-Assessment

From reading this article, I have learned

_____

_____

_____

_____

CRITICAL THINKING

"TODAY'S THE DAY!"

Mel Fisher spent years searching for the treasure from the Spanish galleon Atocha. *At left is some of the treasure he found.*

always wanted to do something adventurous," explained Mel Fisher. According to Fisher, his desire was fueled by reading Robert Louis Stevenson's *Treasure Island* when he was an 11-year-old boy. The image of pirates and sunken treasure thrilled him. Fisher would rush to get all his school work done so he could spend the rest of the day reading about pirates such as Blackbeard and Jean Laffite.

2   Fisher grew up in Indiana—not an ideal place for a boy who loved the sea. But that didn't stop him from experimenting with some underwater diving. One day, he rigged up his own diving helmet. He patched it together out of a 5-gallon paint can and a bicycle pump. He nearly drowned trying it out in a local lake.

3   Fisher grew up to do many things in his life. He built bridges for the U.S. Army during World War II. He worked on his father's chicken ranch in California. He opened the nation's first "dive shop" which supplied divers with lessons and equipment. He raised five children with

his wife and partner, Dolores. Then, in 1962, the whole Fisher family moved to Florida to give treasure hunting a try. It would be a family effort, with Dolores and all the children playing important roles.

4   Treasure hunting is a boom-or-bust business. Most of the time, it's a bust. For his first 360 days at sea, Fisher found nothing. But suddenly, on day 361, business finally boomed. Fisher was testing something he called a "mailbox." It was a device he invented which propelled clear surface water to the bottom of the sea so that divers could see better. The "mailbox" was so powerful it could also dig a hole in the sand on the ocean's bottom. On this lucky day, the hole revealed 1,033 gold coins. "Once you have seen the ocean bottom paved with gold, you'll never forget it," said Fisher. From that moment on, he was hooked for good on treasure hunting.

5   In 1969, Fisher picked up a copy of *Potter's Treasure Diver's Guide*. It described the Spanish galleon *Nuestra Senora de Atocha*. The *Atocha* was the flagship of a 28-vessel fleet. It sank during a hurricane in 1622 while sailing from Cuba to Spain. The *Atocha* went down off the Florida Keys. No one knew exactly where. But ship's records showed that it carried tons of gold and silver headed for the treasuries

of King Philip IV of Spain. This, Fisher decided, was the ship he wanted.

6   For the next 16 years, Fisher searched in vain for the *Atocha*. Every morning he would tell his crew, "Today's the day!" At night, he would tell them, "Tomorrow's the day!" Fisher's optimism seemed almost superhuman. Although he found many small treasures worth millions, he also spent millions to keep his operation going. Treasure hunting is a very expensive business. It costs a small fortune to buy the necessary high-tech equipment and ships. There were times when Fisher had so little money he couldn't pay his crew the money he owed them.

7   Still, he persevered. After reading old Spanish logs, Fisher thought he had the location of the wreck pretty well pinpointed. He figured it probably went down after smashing into a reef off Key West. Fisher believed that the ship remained in one piece. (On this point, he was mistaken. In fact, the ship was broken into many pieces and scattered over 10 miles.) In 1973, Fisher found a tiny bit of the *Atocha* treasure—three silver bars and an anchor. This discovery turned out to be a mixed blessing, however, because these items were seven miles away from where the main treasure was located. "I wish we had never found [the silver bars]," said

Bleth McHaley, a member of Fisher's staff. "It was a false lead that cost us years."

8   The search had a human toll, as well. In 1975, Fisher's oldest son, Dirk, found nine cannons from the *Atocha*. Just one week later, Dirk, his wife Angel, and diver Rick Gage drowned when their salvage

Mel Fisher with some of the treasure he has reclaimed from sunken ships

ship capsized in a storm. This was the only time a deeply-shaken Fisher expressed any doubt about the price he was paying to find the *Atocha*. Still, he decided to go on. "My son would have wanted me to complete the search," Fisher said.

9 It took 10 more years after Dirk's death before Mel Fisher's motto "Today's the day!" came true. By then, Fisher had stopped searching the area where the silver bars had been found. He'd gone back to searching around the reef where he had originally suspected the ship went down. But time seemed to be running out. Once again, Fisher was broke and couldn't pay his crew. Luckily, the crew didn't quit. They believed in Fisher's dream almost as much as he did.

10 Then the big breakthrough came. On the morning of July 20, 1985, Andy Matroci and Greg Wareham began what everyone thought would be just another routine dive. They were checking out some odd shapes on the ocean floor. Wareham, using a metal detector, swam over what looked like large mound covered with lobsters. Suddenly, his metal detector screeched wildly. "It scared the [heck] out of me," said Wareham. That

mysterious mound was nearly solid silver. The two men swam rapidly back to the surface and began waving and shouting, "We're sitting on silver bars! We're sitting on silver bars!"

11 Kane Fisher radioed his father who was in Key West at the time. "Unit 1, this is Unit 11. Put away the charts. We've hit the main pile. We've got the mother lode!"

12 Taffi, Fisher's daughter and a diver, said, "The silver was stacked up like cordwood as far as the eye could see."

13 "It looked just like I dreamed it would," said Shaky Jake, one of 35 divers Fisher employed to bring up the treasure. "There were some rocks and pieces of wood and then bars, bars, bars, bars."

14 The divers also found eight mahogany treasure chests. They looked just like the chests in every treasure hunter's dreams. Seven contained about 2,000 silver coins each. The last one was filled with solid gold bars.

15 It was, in short, the greatest sea treasure ever found. The ship carried more than 600 pounds of gold, 1,038 silver bars, and about 250,000 silver coins. In 1985 terms, the treasure from the *Atocha* was

worth around $400 million. As one crew member jokingly put it, "This means I'll get my paycheck next week."

16 Mel Fisher could only think back to all those fruitless years of searching. He remembered what he had often told his crew when he couldn't pay them. "Just wait until you see the main pile," he would say. "There'll be stacks of silver bars lined up like a brick wall.... There'll be bars of gold and treasure chests filled with gold and silver coins. It's all there, believe me." On July 20, 1985, Mel Fisher finally saw his predictions come true. 🍂

If you have been timed while reading this article, enter your reading time below. Then turn to the Words-per-Minute Table on page 133 and look up your reading speed (words per minute). Enter your reading speed on the graph on page 134.

Reading Time: Lesson 14

_____ : _____
Minutes   Seconds

A | Finding the Main Idea

One statement below expresses the main idea of the article. One statement is too general, or too broad. The other statement explains only part of the article; it is too narrow. Label the statements using the following key:

M—Main Idea   **B—Too Broad**   **N—Too Narrow**

_____ 1. Mel Fisher spent many years searching for sunken treasure and finally found the riches that the galleon *Atocha* had carried to the ocean floor.

_____ 2. The ocean contains incredible treasures: some of them can be uncovered through hard work and faith.

_____ 3. Before Mel Fisher began searching for sunken treasure, he worked on a chicken ranch and opened the first "dive shop" in the United States.

_____ Score 15 points for a correct M answer.

_____ Score 5 points for each correct B or N answer.

_____ **Total Score:** Finding the Main Idea

B | Recalling Facts

How well do you remember the facts in the article? Put an X in the box next to the answer that correctly completes each statement about the article.

1. Mel Fisher grew up in
   - ☐ a. Illinois.
   - ☐ b. Indiana.
   - ☐ c. Florida.

2. The *Atocha* had been carrying
   - ☐ a. soldiers to fight in the Americas, along with guns and swords.
   - ☐ b. slaves.
   - ☐ c. gold and silver.

3. Fisher searched for the *Atocha* for
   - ☐ a. one year.
   - ☐ b. 16 years.
   - ☐ c. 27 years.

4. Fisher's son Dirk died when his
   - ☐ a. plane crashed in Key West.
   - ☐ b. equipment failed to work properly.
   - ☐ c. boat capsized in rough waters.

5. The treasure from the *Atocha* was worth around
   - ☐ a. $20 million.
   - ☐ b. $200 million.
   - ☐ c. $400 million.

Score 5 points for each correct answer.

_____ **Total Score:** Recalling Facts

C | Making Inferences

When you combine your own experience and information from a text to draw a conclusion that is not directly stated in that text, you are making an inference. Below are five statements that may or may not be inferences based on information in the article. Label the statements using the following key:

C—Correct Inference   **F—Faulty Inference**

_____ 1. Mel Fisher made sure that all his children could swim.

_____ 2. Dolores Fisher continually tried to persuade Mel to stop searching for the sunken treasure.

_____ 3. The *Atocha* was the only Spanish ship to sink in the Caribbean Sea while carrying wonderful treasures.

_____ 4. After Fisher found the treasure, he repaid his crew for all their hard work.

_____ 5. Fisher's crew would have left him if they had been able to find other jobs.

> Score 5 points for each correct answer.
>
> _____ **Total Score:** Making Inferences

D | Using Words Precisely

Each numbered sentence below contains an underlined word or phrase from the article. Following the sentence are three definitions. One definition is closest to the meaning of the underlined word. One definition is opposite or nearly opposite. Label those two definitions using the following key. Do not label the remaining definition.

C—Closest   **O—Opposite or Nearly Opposite**

1. Fisher grew up in Indiana—not an <u>ideal</u> place for a boy who loved the sea.

    _____ a. unsuitable

    _____ b. distant

    _____ c. perfect

2. It was a device he invented which <u>propelled</u> clear surface water to the bottom of the sea....

    _____ a. pushed

    _____ b. measured

    _____ c. pulled back

3. For the next 16 years, Fisher searched <u>in vain</u> for the *Atocha*.

    _____ a. angrily

    _____ b. uselessly

    _____ c. productively

4. Still, he [Fisher] <u>persevered</u>.

    _____ a. went broke

    _____ b. kept going

    _____ c. gave up

5. Mel Fisher could only think back to all those <u>fruitless</u> years of searching.

_____ a. profitable

_____ b. exciting

_____ c. unsuccessful

_____ Score 3 points for each correct C answer.

_____ Score 2 points for each correct O answer.

_____ **Total Score:** Using Words Precisely

Enter the four total scores in the spaces below, and add them together to find your Reading Comprehension Score. Then record your score on the graph on page 135.

Score	Question Type	Lesson 14
_____	Finding the Main Idea	
_____	Recalling Facts	
_____	Making Inferences	
_____	Using Words Precisely	
_____	**Reading Comprehension Score**	

Author's Approach

Put an X in the box next to the correct answer.

1. The author uses the first sentence of the article to

☐ a. introduce the reader to the personality of Mel Fisher.

☐ b. show the reader the contrast between Mel Fisher as an adult and as a child.

☐ c. entertain the reader with a funny story about Mel Fisher.

2. Choose the statement below that is the weakest argument for continuing the search for the *Atocha*.

☐ a. It was possible that the search could make those who worked on it very rich.

☐ b. The search was sometimes exciting and fun.

☐ c. The search was dangerous.

3. In this article, "Every morning he [Fisher] would tell his crew, 'Today's the day!'" means

☐ a. Fisher warned the crew that he might give up the search at any time.

☐ b. Fisher began each day with hope that they would find the treasure.

☐ c. Fisher hoped that he and his crew could begin the search that day.

4. The author probably wrote this article in order to

☐ a. describe the beauty of the ocean.

☐ b. raise awareness of the dangers of diving for sunken treasure.

☐ c. tell the story of an incredible discovery and the person who made it happen.

_____ Number of correct answers

Record your personal assessment of your work on the Critical Thinking Chart on page 136.

CRITICAL THINKING

Summarizing and Paraphrasing

Follow the directions provided for question 1. Put an X in the box next to the correct answer for the other questions.

1. Look for the important ideas and events in paragraphs 9 and 10. Summarize those paragraphs in one or two sentences.

_____

_____

_____

2. Read the statement about the article below. Then read the paraphrase of that statement. Choose the reason that best tells why the paraphrase does not say the same thing as the statement.

   Statement: The search for the *Atocha* cost so much that sometimes Fisher was unable to pay his crew.

   Paraphrase: At times, Fisher didn't pay his crew.

   ☐ a.   Paraphrase says too much.

   ☐ b.   Paraphrase doesn't say enough.

   ☐ c.   Paraphrase doesn't agree with the statement about the article.

_____ Number of correct answers

Record your personal assessment of your work on the Critical Thinking Chart on page 136.

Critical Thinking

Put an X in the box next to the correct answer for questions 1, 2, and 4. Follow the directions provided for question 3.

1. Which of the following statements from the article is an opinion rather than a fact?

   ☐ a.   "He [Fisher] raised five children with his wife and partner, Dolores."

   ☐ b.   "Fisher's optimism seemed almost superhuman."

   ☐ c.   "The ship carried more than 600 pounds of gold, 1,038 silver bars, and about 250,000 silver coins."

2. Judging by the events in the article, you can predict that the following will happen next:

   ☐ a.   The Fisher children will become angry with their father for conducting the search.

   ☐ b.   Divers will lose interest in searching for sunken treasure.

   ☐ c.   More people will try to find sunken treasure in the ocean.

3. Choose from the letters below to correctly complete the following statement. Write the letters on the lines.

   On the positive side, _____, but on the negative side _____.

   a.   Mel Fisher found millions of dollars worth of gold and silver

   b.   Mel Fisher was born far from the ocean

   c.   Mel Fisher's oldest son died during the search

4. What was the effect of Fisher's finding three silver bars and an anchor in 1973?

☐ a. Fisher was able to pinpoint the exact location of the *Atocha*.

☐ b. Fisher's crew found the *Atocha* at a different location.

☐ c. Years were lost that could have been spent searching in the right place.

_____ Number of correct answers

Record your personal assessment of your work on the Critical Thinking Chart on page 136.

Self-Assessment

A word or phrase in the article that I do not understand is

_____

_____

_____

_____

Personal Response

Begin the first 5–8 sentences of your own article about finding a sunken or buried treasure. It may tell of a real experience or one that is imagined.

_____

_____

_____

_____

_____

_____

Compare and Contrast

Think about the articles you have read in Unit Two. Pick the four articles that described a discovery or invention in which you would have enjoyed participating. Write their titles in the first column of the chart below. Use information you learned from the articles to fill in the empty boxes in the chart.

Title	Where did the invention or discovery occur?	Who was present at the "Eureka" moment?	What do you think happened immediately after that moment?

Imagine that you were present at one particular discovery from this unit. Describe your feelings. _____

_____

_____

Words-per-Minute Table

Unit Two

Directions: If you were timed while reading an article, refer to the Reading Time you recorded in the box at the end of the article. Use this words-per-minute table to determine your reading speed for that article. Then plot your reading speed on the graph on page 134.

Lesson No. of Words	8 1036	9 922	10 1261	11 1023	12 963	13 997	14 1163	Seconds
1:30	691	615	841	682	642	665	775	**90**
1:40	622	553	757	614	578	598	698	**100**
1:50	565	503	688	558	525	544	634	**110**
2:00	518	461	631	512	482	499	582	**120**
2:10	478	426	582	472	444	460	537	**130**
2:20	444	395	540	438	413	427	498	**140**
2:30	414	369	504	409	385	399	465	**150**
2:40	389	346	473	384	361	374	436	**160**
2:50	366	325	445	361	340	352	410	**170**
3:00	345	307	420	341	321	332	388	**180**
3:10	327	291	398	323	304	315	367	**190**
3:20	311	277	378	307	289	299	349	**200**
3:30	296	263	360	292	275	285	332	**210**
3:40	283	251	344	279	263	272	317	**220**
3:50	270	241	329	267	251	260	303	**230**
4:00	259	231	315	256	241	249	291	**240**
4:10	249	221	303	246	231	239	279	**250**
4:20	239	213	291	236	222	230	268	**260**
4:30	230	205	280	227	214	222	258	**270**
4:40	222	198	270	219	206	214	249	**280**
4:50	214	191	261	212	199	206	241	**290**
5:00	207	184	252	205	193	199	233	**300**
5:10	201	178	244	198	186	193	225	**310**
5:20	194	173	236	192	181	187	218	**320**
5:30	188	168	229	186	175	181	211	**330**
5:40	183	163	223	181	170	176	205	**340**
5:50	178	158	216	175	165	171	199	**350**
6:00	173	154	210	171	161	166	194	**360**
6:10	168	150	204	166	156	162	189	**370**
6:20	164	146	199	162	152	157	184	**380**
6:30	159	142	194	157	148	153	179	**390**
6:40	155	138	189	153	144	150	174	**400**
6:50	152	135	185	150	141	146	170	**410**
7:00	148	132	180	146	138	142	166	**420**
7:10	145	129	176	143	134	139	162	**430**
7:20	141	126	172	140	131	136	159	**440**
7:30	138	123	168	136	128	133	155	**450**
7:40	135	120	164	133	126	130	152	**460**
7:50	132	118	161	131	123	127	148	**470**
8:00	130	115	158	128	120	125	145	**480**

Minutes and Seconds

Plotting Your Progress: Reading Speed

Unit Two

Directions: If you were timed while reading an article, write your words-per-minute rate for that article in the box under the number of the lesson. Then plot your reading speed on the graph by putting a small X on the line directly above the number of the lesson, across from the number of words per minute you read. As you mark your speed for each lesson, graph your progress by drawing a line to connect the X's.

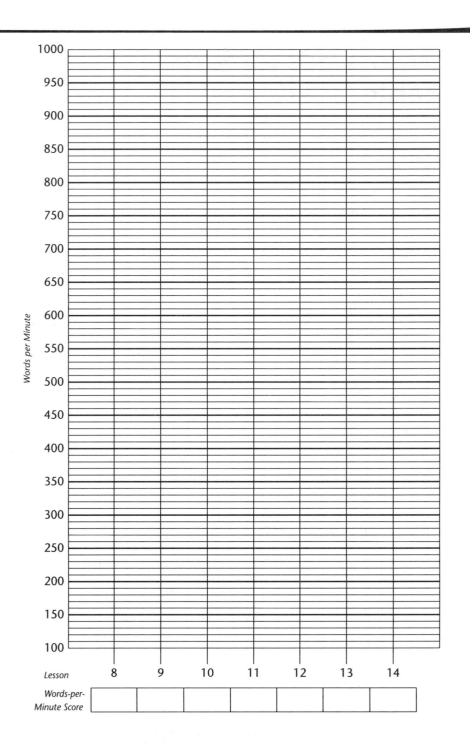

Plotting Your Progress: Reading Comprehension

Unit Two

Directions: Write your Reading Comprehension score for each lesson in the box under the number of the lesson. Then plot your score on the graph by putting a small X on the line directly above the number of the lesson and across from the score you earned. As you mark your score for each lesson, graph your progress by drawing a line to connect the X's.

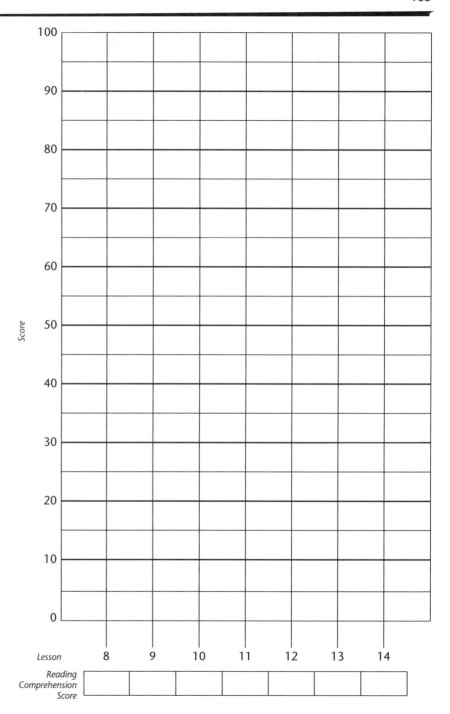

Plotting Your Progress: Critical Thinking

Unit Two

Directions: Work with your teacher to evaluate your responses to the Critical Thinking questions for each lesson. Then fill in the appropriate spaces in the chart below. For each lesson and each type of Critical Thinking question, do the following: Mark a minus sign (–) in the box to indicate areas in which you feel you could improve. Mark a plus sign (+) to indicate areas in which you feel you did well. Mark a minus-slash-plus sign (–/+) to indicate areas in which you had mixed success. Then write any comments you have about your performance, including ideas for improvement.

Lesson	Author's Approach	Summarizing and Paraphrasing	Critical Thinking
8			
9			
10			
11			
12			
13			
14			

UNIT THREE

THE TOMB OF KING TUT

Mr. Howard Carter (left) opening the wall of the inner chamber of the tomb of King Tutankhamen.

On November 4, 1922, archaeologist Howard Carter dragged himself out of bed. Would it be another day of failure in the choking dust and searing heat of Egypt's Valley of the Kings? For 15 years Carter had been searching for the tomb of King Tutankhamen, often called simply King Tut. If he didn't find it soon, he might have to give up.

2   Luckily, however, this day would be different. The workers, who had begun digging earlier that morning, had found something. It was a stone step about six feet long. Carter knew almost immediately that it was part of a sunken staircase. Did it lead to King Tut's tomb? Carter took that day and the next to dig—carefully and slowly—down to the 12th step. There he found a doorway. The seals on the outer door, made 3,000 years earlier, proved it was a royal tomb and that its contents were intact.

3   Excitedly, Carter sent an urgent telegram to his financial backer and partner, Lord Carnarvon, who was in England. "At last have made wonderful discovery in Valley. Congratulations," he wrote. Carter knew that Carnarvon would

want to share in the thrill of opening and entering the tomb. So he covered the stairway with dirt again to protect the tomb from thieves and waited for Lord Carnarvon's arrival.

4   Eighteen days later Lord Carnarvon arrived from England. The two men began uncovering the stairway once more. On November 25, they reached the outer door of the tomb. The next day they arrived at the inner door. "Feverishly," Carter later wrote, "we cleared away the remaining last scraps of rubbish on the floor of the passage before the doorway." They then saw the royal seal of Tutankhamen pressed into the plaster. There was no mistake—this was it! Carter's years of toil and failure had turned into triumph. "The day of days," were the words Carter used to describe this moment, "the most wonderful that I have ever lived through."

5   Fighting to control his excitement, Carter used a knife to make a small hole in the top of the door. He took a lighted candle and peered inside. "At first I could see nothing…, but presently, as my eyes grew accustomed to the light, details of the room emerged slowly from the mist, strange animals, statues and gold—everywhere the glint of gold."

6   Carter stood in awed silence. "For the moment—an eternity it must have seemed to the others standing by—I was struck dumb with amazement."

7   Lord Carnarvon, unable to stand the suspense any longer, called out from behind Carter, "Can you see anything?"

8   "Yes, it is wonderful," was all Carter could say.

9   Howard Carter had unearthed the greatest treasure ever found in Egypt. The four rock-hewn rooms held more than 5,000 objects. It took Carter two months to reach the highlight of his discovery—the burial room. There he found a solid 22-carat gold coffin weighing 2,448 pounds. He also found what is now the most famous item in the tomb—the extraordinary golden mask which covered King Tut's mummified head.

10   As was the custom in his day, King Tutankhamen had been buried with everything he might need to make him happy in the afterlife. His tomb was crammed with games, lamps, boats, jars of honey, flowers, statues of gods and goddesses, bows and arrows, baskets, jewels, clothes, and chairs. The tomb also contained two golden chariots which were so large they had to be taken apart to fit into the tomb. He was even buried with a lock of his grandmother's hair. Carter wrote, "So crowded [was the tomb] that it was a matter of extreme difficulty to move

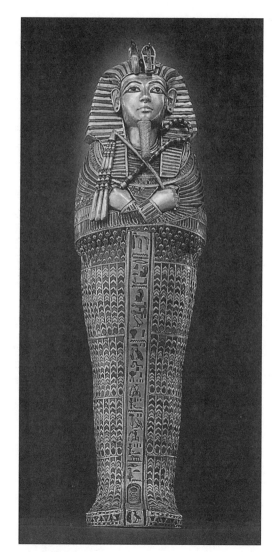

King Tut's legendary golden coffin

one [precious item] without running serious risk of damaging others." Searchers worked patiently and carefully for 10 years to excavate the entire tomb. The contents of the tomb are now on display at the Egyptian Museum in Cairo.

11   While other pharaohs had similar tombs, these other resting places had all been robbed eons ago. King Tut's was the only tomb that was left almost completely untouched. The tomb of King Tutankhamen actually had been robbed once or twice, but those robberies had occurred soon after the king was laid to rest. The thieves, it seemed, were either frightened away or acted in such fear that they took only some oils and a few small items of jewelry. In their haste, the robbers had dropped some of their booty on the floor. After these early break-ins, Egyptian officials resealed Tut's tomb. It then remained undisturbed for more than 3,000 years.

12   Why was this tomb left alone? One theory is that King Tutankhamen was only a minor figure in Egyptian history. He came to the throne in 1352 B.C. and died nine years later at the age of 18. Perhaps big-time grave robbers passed

over his tomb for the riches of more tempting targets. Or perhaps his underground tomb was too well covered to be noticed. After all, the tomb of another pharaoh, Ramses VI, was built right next door just 200 years later. During the building of Ramses's tomb, workers lived in huts erected over King Tut's tomb. The huts later fell to rubble, obscuring King Tut's burial site. In addition, much of the dirt for Ramses's tomb was dumped on the entrance to Tut's tomb.

13   When Carter began his excavation of Tut's tomb, some people proclaimed that breaking into it would bring bad luck. Dire inscriptions etched on the tomb warned that anyone who disturbed the king's tomb would be punished. The newspapers in London dubbed the warning "The Curse of the Pharaoh." And in fact, barely six weeks after the discovery of Tutankhamen's tomb, Lord Carnarvon died. He died from a mosquito bite which caused a blood infection. There's more. During the night Carnarvon lay dying in Cairo, the city went black from a mysterious power failure. At the same time, back in London, Carnarvon's dog

gave a weird howl and then rolled over dead. Over the years, there were other deaths and suicides among people linked to the tomb.

14   Still, Howard Carter himself said that the "curse" was nonsense. If anyone was going to be cursed, he figured, it should have been him. But the great archaeologist died of natural causes at the age of 64 in his home in London on March 2, 1939. 🍃

If you have been timed while reading this article, enter your reading time below. Then turn to the Words-per-Minute Table on page 195 and look up your reading speed (words per minute). Enter your reading speed on the graph on page 196.

Reading Time: **Lesson 15**

_____ : _____
Minutes   Seconds

A **Finding the Main Idea**

One statement below expresses the main idea of the article. One statement is too general, or too broad. The other statement explains only part of the article; it is too narrow. Label the statements using the following key:

M—Main Idea   **B—Too Broad**   **N—Too Narrow**

_____ 1. Egypt is the site of a number of ancient wonders.

_____ 2. The 1922 discovery of the tomb of King Tut by determined archaeologists yielded unimaginable treasures.

_____ 3. After entering the tomb of King Tut, Howard Carter was so amazed by its splendor that he could not speak for a few minutes.

_____ Score 15 points for a correct M answer.

_____ Score 5 points for each correct B or N answer.

_____ **Total Score:** Finding the Main Idea

B **Recalling Facts**

How well do you remember the facts in the article? Put an X in the box next to the answer that correctly completes each statement about the article.

1. The door of King Tut's tomb was decorated with
   ☐ a. gold letters.
   ☐ b. jewels.
   ☐ c. the royal seal.

2. The most famous item found in the tomb was
   ☐ a. a golden mask that had covered King Tut's head.
   ☐ b. King Tut's grandmother's hair.
   ☐ c. a chariot.

3. Most items from the tomb are on display at the
   ☐ a. Smithsonian Institution in Washington, D.C.
   ☐ b. British Museum in London.
   ☐ c. Egyptian Museum in Cairo.

4. King Tut died at the age of around
   ☐ a. nine.
   ☐ b. 18.
   ☐ c. 64.

5. Lord Carnarvon died of
   ☐ a. an infection brought on by a mosquito bite.
   ☐ b. injuries he received in a fall in the tomb.
   ☐ c. a virus he picked up from the stale tomb air.

Score 5 points for each correct answer.

_____ **Total Score:** Recalling Facts

C | Making Inferences

When you combine your own experience and information from a text to draw a conclusion that is not directly stated in that text, you are making an inference. Below are five statements that may or may not be inferences based on information in the article. Label the statements using the following key:

C—Correct Inference   **F—Faulty Inference**

_____ 1. King Tut was the most beloved of all Egyptian rulers.

_____ 2. Lord Carnarvon was as excited about the discovery as Howard Carter was.

_____ 3. For years, no one except Carter and Carnarvon knew about the discovery.

_____ 4. King Tut's tomb is located in the middle of a large, modern city.

_____ 5. Lord Carnarvon always resented the fact that he had not been able to enter the tomb before Carter.

Score 5 points for each correct answer.

_____ **Total Score:** Making Inferences

D | Using Words Precisely

Each numbered sentence below contains an underlined word or phrase from the article. Following the sentence are three definitions. One definition is closest to the meaning of the underlined word. One definition is opposite or nearly opposite. Label those two definitions using the following key. Do not label the remaining definition.

C—Closest   **O—Opposite or Nearly Opposite**

1. Excitedly, Carter sent an <u>urgent</u> telegram to his financial backer and partner, Lord Carnarvon, who was in England.

_____ a. asking for immediate attention

_____ b. unimportant

_____ c. long

2. Searchers worked patiently and carefully for 10 years to <u>excavate</u> the entire tomb.

_____ a. bury

_____ b. learn about

_____ c. uncover

3. In their <u>haste</u>, the robbers had dropped some of their booty on the floor.

_____ a. fear

_____ b. hurry

_____ c. slow pace

4. The huts later fell to rubble, <u>obscuring</u> King Tut's burial site.

_____ a. hiding

_____ b. destroying

_____ c. exposing, uncovering

5. <u>Dire</u> inscriptions etched on the tomb warned that anyone who disturbed the king's tomb would be punished.

_____ a. ancient

_____ b. cheerful

_____ c. dreadful

_____ Score 3 points for each correct C answer.

_____ Score 2 points for each correct O answer.

_____ **Total Score:** Using Words Precisely

Enter the four total scores in the spaces below, and add them together to find your Reading Comprehension Score. Then record your score on the graph on page 197.

Score	Question Type	Lesson 15
_____	Finding the Main Idea	
_____	Recalling Facts	
_____	Making Inferences	
_____	Using Words Precisely	
_____	**Reading Comprehension Score**	

Author's Approach

Put an X in the box next to the correct answer.

1. What is the author's purpose in writing "The Tomb of King Tut"?

☐ a. To encourage the reader to become an archaeologist

☐ b. To inform the reader about a wonderful discovery

☐ c. To persuade the reader to visit Egypt

2. Which of the following statements from the article best describes Carter's first reaction to the sights he saw after entering the tomb?

☐ a. "Carter stood in awed silence."

☐ b. "Carter knew that Carnarvon would want to share in the thrill of opening and entering the tomb."

☐ c. "Still, Howard Carter himself said that the 'curse' was nonsense."

3. Judging by statements from the article "The Tomb of King Tut," you can conclude that the author wants the reader to think that

☐ a. the fact that Howard Carter died of natural causes at the age of 64 proves that there is no curse attached to King Tut's tomb.

☐ b. Lord Carnarvon's death was caused by the "Curse of the Pharaoh."

☐ c. The mosquito that bit Lord Carnarvon came from King Tut's tomb.

CRITICAL THINKING

4. Choose the statement below that is the weakest argument for believing in the "Curse of the Pharaoh."

☐ a. Lord Carnarvon died barely six weeks after the discovery of the tomb of King Tut.

☐ b. The lights mysteriously went out in Cairo on the night that Carnarvon died.

☐ c. Howard Carter lived for many years after the discovery and died of natural causes at the age of 64.

_____ Number of correct answers

Record your personal assessment of your work on the Critical Thinking Chart on page 198.

Summarizing and Paraphrasing

Put an X in the box next to the correct answer.

1. Below are summaries of the article. Choose the summary that says all the most important things about the article but in the fewest words.

☐ a. The young King Tutankhamen was buried in a grand tomb along with every luxury he might need in the afterlife.

☐ b. Howard Carter and his financial backer, Lord Carnarvon, searched for years for King Tut's tomb. Their persistence was rewarded in 1922 when they found the tomb filled with treasures. King Tut's tomb was still mostly intact after 3,000 years.

☐ c. King Tut's tomb was the only tomb in Egypt's Valley of the Kings that had not been robbed since ancient times. The only time it was robbed, the thieves took only a few items before they ran out.

2. Choose the sentence that correctly restates the following sentence from the article:

"The seals on the outer door, made 3,000 years earlier, proved it was a royal tomb and that its contents were intact."

☐ a. The searchers hoped that the tomb was still intact, and they were dismayed to find seals on the outer door.

☐ b. The seals on the door might have suggested that the searchers were about to enter a royal tomb.

☐ c. Seeing the sealed door, searchers knew that the tomb had belonged to royalty and its contents had not been touched, even after 3,000 years.

_____ Number of correct answers

Record your personal assessment of your work on the Critical Thinking Chart on page 198.

Critical Thinking

Follow the directions provided for questions 1, 2, and 4. Put an X in the box next to the correct answer for question 3.

1. For each statement below, write O if it expresses an opinion or write F if it expresses a fact.

_____ a. Howard Carter had been searching for King Tut's tomb for 15 years when he finally found it.

_____ b. King Tut had been buried with games, lamps, boats, and even a pair of golden chariots.

_____ c. It was inappropriate that English, not Egyptian, archaeologists were the first people to enter King Tut's tomb after 3,000 years.

2. Think about cause-effect relationships in the article. Fill in the blanks in the cause-effect chart, drawing from the letters below.

Cause	Effect
_____	Carnarvon died in six weeks.
Carter uncovered a stone step.	_____
_____	King Tut's tomb was almost intact.

a. He knew that he had found a sunken staircase.

b. Robbers hadn't entered the tomb in 3,000 years.

c. Carnarvon was bitten by a mosquito and developed an infection.

3. How is the finding of King Tut's tomb related to the theme of this book?

☐ a. King Tut had been the ruler of Egypt.

☐ b. The tomb was located in the Valley of Kings.

☐ c. Carter and Carnarvon unearthed a wonderful treasure that had been hidden for 3,000 years.

4. Which paragraphs from the article provide evidence that supports your answer to question 2?

_____

_____ Number of correct answers

Record your personal assessment of your work on the Critical Thinking Chart on page 198.

Personal Response

How do you think you would feel if you found a treasure like the tomb of King Tut?

_____

_____

_____

_____

Self-Assessment

I'm proud of how I answered question # _____ in section _____ because

_____

_____

_____

_____

CRITICAL THINKING

A BRILLIANT BLUNDER

A worker in a modern rubber manufacturing plant guides a sheet of crude rubber onto a pallet.

He was in and out of debtors' prison so often he should have had his own key. Whenever he walked down the street, even his friends would cross to the other side to avoid him. Once he was so desperate for money that he hocked his own children's schoolbooks to get five dollars. To be perfectly blunt, Charles Goodyear was one of life's losers. And yet this oddball character accidentally invented something that profoundly changed the way we all live today.

2   Goodyear was born in 1800, and it was pretty much downhill from there. He got his first real job working in his father's hardware manufacturing business. By 1830, Charles had helped drive his father into bankruptcy. That same year, the young Goodyear got his first look at the inside of a debtors' prison.

3   In 1834, while in New York City, Goodyear wandered into a branch of the Roxbury India Rubber Company. The company had rubber life preservers for sale. They weren't very good products, but Goodyear bought one anyway. After a few days, Goodyear returned to the store with a design for a better valve for the life

preserver. The manager was unimpressed. Frankly, he told Goodyear, it would have been better if he had improved the rubber itself.

4   Rubber had been around for centuries. Christopher Columbus found Native Americans playing games with rubber balls. The rubber they used for the balls came from plants and trees in the form of a white fluid called latex. Much later, French explorers found Peruvian Indians making boots from the sap of a native tree. A sample of this "gum elastic" was given to a famous British scientist named Joseph Priestley. He discovered that it was excellent for rubbing out pencil mistakes on paper. So Priestley renamed the gum "rubber."

5   For years, rubber remained little more than a curiosity for most people. Then, in the early 1830s, rubber products made a brief splash in the United States. Several companies sprang up to produce goods such as life preservers, coats, boots, shoes, and wagon covers out of rubber. There was, however, one major problem: the rubber couldn't stand up to changes in temperature. On hot summer days it melted, leaving gummy masses that smelled so bad they had to be buried. In the winter, cold air turned the rubber hard as a rock and so brittle that it broke into pieces. Within a couple of years, all companies trying to manufacture rubber products were out of business.

6   Following that brief period, most people gave up on rubber. But not Charles Goodyear. He continued to believe that the substance could be useful. If he could just figure out how to make rubber impervious to heat and cold, he could make a fortune. Needless to say, that was a huge "if," but Goodyear was convinced it could be done. He simply needed to find the right additive.

7   Although he had no training in chemistry, Goodyear set about finding the magic formula that would make rubber both resilient and strong. To finance his experiments, he borrowed money from friends and other investors. Then, using a rolling pin, a marble slab, and a few pots and pans, he began mixing rubber with everything his kitchen had to offer. He tried ink, cream cheese, witch hazel, castor oil, and soup, but nothing worked. Still, he kept at it.

8   Meanwhile, Goodyear's financial situation remained grim. A friend once described the pitiful Goodyear this way: "If you meet a man who has on an India rubber cap, stock, coat, vest, and shoes, with an India rubber money purse *without a cent of money in it, that is he.*" Goodyear's faith in the possibilities of rubber, however, was unshaken. Even when he was sent back to prison he continued his experiments. He just had his wife bring the rubber and new potential additives to him in his cell.

9   At last, in 1839, Goodyear solved the mystery. At least, he *thought* he solved the

Charles Goodyear, American rubber experimenter

mystery. He found that the key was to mix rubber with magnesia and quicklime. That combination made the rubber smooth and supple. When Goodyear proudly announced his discovery to the press, the public began to share his excitement. The government even gave him a contract to make rubber mailbags. But Goodyear and his supporters were in for a deep disappointment. The rubber concoction he had cooked up did not last. The rubber mailbags disintegrated if even a drop of lemonade or any other mild acid was spilled on them.

10   Despite this setback, the resolute Goodyear refused to quit. Back in his kitchen in Woburn, Massachusetts, he mixed up another batch of rubber, this time using sulfur in the blend. Amazingly, when he accidentally spilled some of it on a hot stove, it didn't melt; it charred. When the blob cooled, Goodyear found that the rubber wasn't sticky at all. "I...inferred that if the charring...could be stopped at the right moment," Goodyear wrote, "it might divest the compound of its stickiness throughout." Goodyear had,

in fact, discovered the secret of rubber. He called his new process "vulcanization" after the Roman god of fire, Vulcan.

11   Unfortunately, Goodyear had burned too many bridges with his past failures. No one wanted to support him anymore. It took him five years just to win a patent for vulcanization. By then, the news of his success had begun to spread. Other people now wanted to manufacture rubber goods. To do so, they needed Goodyear's permission to use vulcanization. Desperate for cash, he sold manufacturing licenses for far less than they were worth.

12   And so while others made a fortune off his rubber process, Charles Goodyear continued to struggle. He lived long enough to see his invention spark a major industry, and he achieved enough recognition so that after his death the Goodyear Tire Company adopted his name. (Ironically, although Goodyear had dozens of ideas about new rubber products, he never thought of inflatable tires.) Still, Charles Goodyear couldn't make a buck for himself. He just sank deeper and deeper in debt.

13   In 1855, Napoleon III, the emperor of France, was impressed by Goodyear's rubber exhibition at a world's fair in Paris. Napoleon wanted to award him the Grand Medal of Honor and the Cross of the Legion of Honor. But where was the inventor? Napoleon was startled to find him languishing in a debtors' prison on the outskirts of Paris. When Goodyear died in 1860, he was more than $200,000 in debt. 🍃

If you have been timed while reading this article, enter your reading time below. Then turn to the Words-per-Minute Table on page 195 and look up your reading speed (words per minute). Enter your reading speed on the graph on page 196.

Reading Time: Lesson 16

_____ : _____

Minutes   Seconds

A | Finding the Main Idea

One statement below expresses the main idea of the article. One statement is too general, or too broad. The other statement explains only part of the article; it is too narrow. Label the statements using the following key:

M—Main Idea   **B—Too Broad**   **N—Too Narrow**

_____ 1. Although Charles Goodyear was a failure at business, he was a successful inventor who accidentally discovered vulcanization, the secret to making rubber useful.

_____ 2. Charles Goodyear combined ink, cream cheese, and soup with rubber in his search for a way to make useable rubber.

_____ 3. Many times, great inventions result from lucky accidents.

_____ Score 15 points for a correct M answer.

_____ Score 5 points for each correct B or N answer.

_____ **Total Score:** Finding the Main Idea

B | Recalling Facts

How well do you remember the facts in the article? Put an X in the box next to the answer that correctly completes each statement about the article.

1. Charles Goodyear's first real job was
   - ☐ a. manufacturing products made from rubber.
   - ☐ b. inventing products.
   - ☐ c. helping his father in his hardware manufacturing business.

2. According to the article, Peruvian Indians used rubber to make
   - ☐ a. boots.
   - ☐ b. balls.
   - ☐ c. erasers.

3. In hot weather, pure rubber
   - ☐ a. melted and smelled bad.
   - ☐ b. became hard and brittle.
   - ☐ c. disintegrated into little pieces.

4. Vulcanizing rubber means
   - ☐ a. heating it to the proper temperature.
   - ☐ b. combining it with castor oil.
   - ☐ c. mixing it with magnesia and quicklime.

5. After Goodyear invented vulcanization, he
   - ☐ a. became rich.
   - ☐ b. remained poor.
   - ☐ c. was totally forgotten.

Score 5 points for each correct answer.

_____ **Total Score:** Recalling Facts

C | Making Inferences

When you combine your own experience and information from a text to draw a conclusion that is not directly stated in that text, you are making an inference. Below are five statements that may or may not be inferences based on information in the article. Label the statements using the following key:

C—Correct Inference   F—Faulty Inference

_____ 1. Charles Goodyear was persistent and single-minded in pursuit of a goal.

_____ 2. The balls that Columbus saw the Native Americans playing with became sticky when the weather got hot.

_____ 3. All successful inventors have a background in college, or at least high school, chemistry.

_____ 4. The Goodyear kitchen was usually in a state of disorder.

_____ 5. Charles Goodyear was familiar with the stories of Roman gods and goddesses.

Score 5 points for each correct answer.

_____ **Total Score:** Making Inferences

D | Using Words Precisely

Each numbered sentence below contains an underlined word or phrase from the article. Following the sentence are three definitions. One definition is closest to the meaning of the underlined word. One definition is opposite or nearly opposite. Label those two definitions using the following key. Do not label the remaining definition.

C—Closest   O—Opposite or Nearly Opposite

1. And yet this oddball character accidentally invented something that <u>profoundly</u> changed the way we all live today.

_____ a. just barely

_____ b. surprisingly

_____ c. thoroughly

2. If he could just figure out how to make rubber <u>impervious to</u> heat and cold, he could make a fortune.

_____ a. greatly changed by

_____ b. unaffected by

_____ c. separate from

3. That combination made rubber smooth and <u>supple</u>.

_____ a. light

_____ b. stiff and unbending

_____ c. flexible

4. Despite this setback, the <u>resolute</u> Goodyear refused to quit.

_____ a. determined

_____ b. clever

_____ c. easily discouraged

5. Napoleon was startled to find him <u>languishing</u> in a debtors' prison on the outskirts of Paris.

_____ a. prospering

_____ b. wasting away

_____ c. visiting

_____ Score 3 points for each correct C answer.

_____ Score 2 points for each correct O answer.

_____ **Total Score:** Using Words Precisely

Enter the four total scores in the spaces below, and add them together to find your Reading Comprehension Score. Then record your score on the graph on page 197.

Score	Question Type	Lesson 16
_____	Finding the Main Idea	
_____	Recalling Facts	
_____	Making Inferences	
_____	Using Words Precisely	
_____	**Reading Comprehension Score**	

Author's Approach

Put an X in the box next to the correct answer.

1. What does the author mean by the statement "Goodyear was born in 1800, and it was pretty much downhill from there"?

☐ a. Although Goodyear's birth was difficult, the rest of his life was easy.

☐ b. Goodyear's life got easier and easier as he grew older.

☐ c. Goodyear's life was not too pleasant and had few high points.

2. The main purpose of the first paragraph is to

☐ a. present an overview of the article to come.

☐ b. make the reader feel distaste for Charles Goodyear.

☐ c. introduce the reader to the concept of debtors' prison.

3. From the statements below, choose those that you believe the author would agree with.

☐ a. It is kind of sad that Goodyear didn't benefit from his discovery.

☐ b. Most people treated Goodyear unfairly throughout his life.

☐ c. Charles Goodyear was an unusual person.

4. The author tells this story mainly by

☐ a. telling about events in the order they happened.

☐ b. comparing different topics.

☐ c. using his or her imagination and creativity.

_____ Number of correct answers

Record your personal assessment of your work on the Critical Thinking Chart on page 198.

Summarizing and Paraphrasing

Follow the directions provided for questions 1 and 2.

1. Look for the important ideas and events in paragraphs 11 and 12. Summarize those paragraphs in one or two sentences.

_____

_____

_____

2. Complete the following one-sentence summary of the article using the lettered phrases from the phrase bank below. Write the letters on the lines.

Phrase Bank:
a. Goodyear's situation at the end of his life
b. a description of Goodyear's early life
c. Goodyear's attempts to make rubber impervious to temperature and his success

After a short introduction, the article about Charles Goodyear begins with _____, goes on to explain _____, and ends with _____.

_____ Number of correct answers

Record your personal assessment of your work on the Critical Thinking Chart on page 198.

Critical Thinking

Put an X in the box next to the correct answer for questions 1, 4, and 5. Follow the directions provided for the other questions.

1. Which of the following statements from the article is an opinion rather than a fact?
   - ☐ a. "When the blob cooled, Goodyear found that the rubber wasn't sticky at all."
   - ☐ b. "To be perfectly blunt, Charles Goodyear was one of life's losers."
   - ☐ c. "In the winter, cold air turned the rubber hard as a rock and so brittle that it broke into pieces."

2. Choose from the letters below to correctly complete the following statement. Write the letters on the lines.

   On the positive side, _____, but on the negative side _____.
   a. Goodyear had no formal training in chemistry
   b. Goodyear himself never benefited from his discovery
   c. Goodyear's discovery improved life for us all

3. Read paragraph 10. Then choose from the letters below to correctly complete the following statement. Write the letters on the lines.

   According to paragraph 10, _____ because _____.
   a. Goodyear discovered vulcanization
   b. Goodyear named his process after the god of fire
   c. Goodyear dropped a blob on his stove and it charred instead of melting

4. If you were an inventor, how could you use the information in the article to help you find the answers to problems you are working on?

☐ a. Like Goodyear, borrow from your friends.

☐ b. Like Goodyear, pay attention to unusual events, even if they are accidental.

☐ c. Like Goodyear, work in your kitchen.

5. What did you have to do to answer question 3?

☐ a. find a cause (why something happened)

☐ b. find a description (how something looks)

☐ c. draw a conclusion (a sensible statement based on the text and your experience)

_____ Number of correct answers

Record your personal assessment of your work on the Critical Thinking Chart on page 198.

Personal Response

This article is different from other articles about inventions or discoveries I've read because

_____

_____

_____

_____

and Charles Goodyear is unlike other inventors because

_____

_____

_____

_____

Self-Assessment

The part I found most difficult about the article was

_____

_____

_____

_____

I found this difficult because

_____

_____

_____

_____

CRITICAL THINKING

THE KLONDIKE GOLD RUSH

George Carmack tossed and turned in his sleep. For days he and his buddies, Skookum Jim and Tagish Charlie, had been panning Rabbit Creek for gold. Their luck hadn't been very good. Then, according to legend, Carmack had a powerful and mystical dream in which he saw a king salmon swimming through the rushing water with gleaming eyes made from gold nuggets.

2   Perhaps this dream spurred Carmack to pan a new spot in the river. Or perhaps it simply inspired him to look harder at the scrabbly pebbles in the river bed. In any case, soon after he had this dream, Carmack's life changed forever.

3   It was August 1896. The three prospectors were living in Canada's Yukon Territory just east of Alaska. In those days, many people across North America spent their time looking for gold. Only a few, though, did it in this forlorn corner of the continent. Skookum Jim and Tagish Charlie were natives of the Yukon. They were members of the Tagish Athabascan people. Carmack was a veteran prospector from California who had married Jim's sister, Kate.

The famous Chilkoot Pass in the Yukon was also known as the Golden Staircase. This was part of the overland route to the gold fields in the Klondike.

4   August 17 began like any other day for the three men. They were working a tributary of the Klondike River known as Rabbit Creek. All at once, they noticed some enticing traces of gold in the creek. With their pulses racing, they followed the traces to a place where the bedrock lay exposed. There they found a small nugget of gold. As the men turned over loose pieces of rock, they found more gold—lots more—in the cracks. As Carmack later said, the gold was "thick between the flaky slabs, like cheese sandwiches." As a result of their discovery, the name "Rabbit Creek" would soon be changed to "Bonanza Creek."

5   The next day, the three men staked their claims, ensuring they could keep whatever gold they found in that part of the river. News of their good fortune spread quickly throughout the Yukon. Over the next few days, gold prospectors swarmed over the entire region around the Klondike River.

6   Newlyweds Ethel and Clarence Berry happened to be in Bill McPhee's saloon when Carmack walked in and announced his discovery. The Berrys quickly jumped on a dog sled and dashed off to seek their fortune, staking their claims on Eldorado Creek. On August 31, a huge vein of gold was found on this tiny creek. The vein eventually yielded gold valued at more than $500 million today. The Berrys both grew very wealthy and Ethel became world famous as "The Bride of the Klondike."

7   Although the discovery of gold was big news in the Yukon, it took a while for word to spread to the outside world. That's because the Yukon was, and remains, one of the most remote areas of the world. By the summer of 1897, though, everyone knew the Klondike was the place to be. If anyone doubted it, those doubts were erased on July 14, 1897. That's when the steamship *Excelsior* pulled into San Francisco harbor bearing more than half a million dollars worth of Klondike gold. Three days later, the steamship *Portland* docked in Seattle. Aboard were 68 miners carrying about $1 million worth of gold.

8   Reporters rushed to print the news. One newspaper proclaimed: "SHIP'S IN WITH A TON OF SOLID GOLD ON BOARD," while a banner headline on another announced: "GOLD EVERY-WHERE!" One writer claimed that the size of the Klondike gold fields rivaled Amer-

Broadway, the main street in Skagway, Alaska, in 1898

ica's wheat fields and that the yellow streams of gold were as vast as the country's amber waves of grain. Rumors spread of nuggets the size of apples just waiting to be picked up off the ground.

9   And so began the great Klondike Gold Rush of 1897 and 1898. People from all walks of life—artists, doctors, gamblers, ministers, teachers—caught gold fever. In all, more than 100,000 dreamers set out for the Yukon. Only about one third of these so-called "stampeders" made it, however. Most, driven only by gold fever, began their quest without a clue of what hazards lay along the way. The Yukon certainly has its natural charm and beauty, but it also has raging rivers, imposing mountains, and temperatures that often fall to –50 degrees Fahrenheit. These proved to be formidable barriers to the folks who headed north looking for gold.

10   Stampeders had their choice of several possible routes to the gold fields, each undesirable in its own way. Those with time and money could take the all-water route. This was generally considered to be the safest path. The route involved taking a steamboat from Seattle or other some other West Coast port to the Yukon River. Next, people had to board a boat for the 1,500-mile journey up the Yukon River. The ride ended at Dawson, an old Indian fishing camp that was now a boom town with two banks, two newspapers, five churches, 20 saloons, and 30,000 people.

11   Many travelers, however, discovered that the promised boats did not exist. Unscrupulous con men simply pocketed people's fare and then disappeared. Those boats that did exist often got off to a late start. When the winter closed in, the boats and their passengers were caught in the river's ice.

12   Poorer stampeders had to take their chances on foot, using one of the overland routes. Many began their arduous trek at Skagway or Kyea, Alaska. Skagway wasn't a wise choice for one reason—Soapy Smith. Smith was a gangster from Denver, Colorado, who brought his gang of 300 thugs up to prey upon naive stampeders. Smith's men robbed and shot prospectors indiscriminately. Sam Steele, a North-West Mounted Police officer said, "Neither law nor order prevailed. Honest persons had no protection from the gang of rascals who plied their nefarious trade. Might was right; murder, robbery and petty theft were common occurrences." And that was before the stampeders even hit the trail!

13   Some would-be prospectors took the Chilkoot Pass, an old Tlingit trading route. The trail was nearly vertical in places. The prospectors, carrying their supplies on their back, had to scale up the mountain in a solemn single file that frequently stretched for miles. In the spring of 1898, an avalanche killed over 60 people on this trail.

14   Others took the infamous White Pass, a crude and narrow trail. Not as steep as Chilkoot trail, this route became known as Dead Horse Trail because so many horses perished on it. Stampeders drove their pack animals so hard that the poor creatures either died in falls or dropped dead from starvation or exhaustion. Some people went crazy on the Dead Horse Trail from the overpowering stench of dead horse flesh. Others died from a raging fever caused by eating the rotten meat of the dead horses.

15   Most of those who did finally make it to the Klondike gold fields saw their dreams end in disappointment. The best claims had already been staked out by local people. A few stampeders got lucky and found their fortune; a few others stayed on in the Yukon and earned a living doing other things. But most fled the region within a year or two. When the word came that gold had been discovered in Nome, Alaska, many set off for there. By 1899, life in the Yukon was pretty much back to normal. Yet despite its grim death toll and short life span, the Great Klondike Gold Rush will always be counted as one of the greatest gold rushes in history. 🍂

If you have been timed while reading this article, enter your reading time below. Then turn to the Words-per-Minute Table on page 195 and look up your reading speed (words per minute). Enter your reading speed on the graph on page 196.

Reading Time: Lesson 17

_____ : _____

Minutes   Seconds

A | Finding the Main Idea

One statement below expresses the main idea of the article. One statement is too general, or too broad. The other statement explains only part of the article; it is too narrow. Label the statements using the following key:

M—Main Idea   **B—Too Broad**   **N—Too Narrow**

_____ 1. George Carmack and his family's discovery of gold in a remote area called the Klondike caused a tremendous, historic rush for gold that lasted for almost three years.

_____ 2. It seems that wherever gold is found, people rush in, hoping they will get rich, too.

_____ 3. Ethel and Clarence Berry were among the lucky prospectors who made millions of dollars in the Klondike.

_____ Score 15 points for a correct M answer.

_____ Score 5 points for each correct B or N answer.

_____ **Total Score:** Finding the Main Idea

B | Recalling Facts

How well do you remember the facts in the article? Put an X in the box next to the answer that correctly completes each statement about the article.

1. The Yukon Territory is located in
    - ☐ a. Canada.
    - ☐ b. Alaska.
    - ☐ c. California.

2. After prospector George Carmack's discovery, Rabbit Creek was renamed
    - ☐ a. Carmack Creek.
    - ☐ b. Gold Creek.
    - ☐ c. Bonanza Creek.

3. On July 14, 1897, the steamship *Excelsior* docked in San Francisco with gold worth about
    - ☐ a. $100 million.
    - ☐ b. half a million dollars.
    - ☐ c. $5 million.

4. The safest way to the Klondike was
    - ☐ a. the all-water route.
    - ☐ b. the overland route through Skagway.
    - ☐ c. through Chilkoot Pass.

5. Soapy Smith was a
    - ☐ a. local prospector who found millions of dollars worth of gold in the Klondike.
    - ☐ b. gangster from Denver, Colorado.
    - ☐ c. North-West Mounted Police officer.

Score 5 points for each correct answer.

_____ **Total Score:** Recalling Facts

Making Inferences

When you combine your own experience and information from a text to draw a conclusion that is not directly stated in that text, you are making an inference. Below are five statements that may or may not be inferences based on information in the article. Label the statements using the following key:

C—Correct Inference   F—Faulty Inference

_____ 1. If gold were found in a remote part of the world today, no one would care.

_____ 2. Ethel and Clarence Berry acted quickly once they got an idea.

_____ 3. Exciting newspaper reports contributed to the intensity of the Klondike gold rush.

_____ 4. Soapy Smith was tried and convicted for his criminal activities.

_____ 5. Many travelers learned that the safest time to pay for a boat trip is after you reach your destination.

Score 5 points for each correct answer.

_____ **Total Score:** Making Inferences

D **Using Words Precisely**

Each numbered sentence below contains an underlined word or phrase from the article. Following the sentence are three definitions. One definition is closest to the meaning of the underlined word. One definition is opposite or nearly opposite. Label those two definitions using the following key. Do not label the remaining definition.

C—Closest   O—Opposite or Nearly Opposite

1. Only a few, though, did it in this <u>forlorn</u> corner of the continent.

   _____ a. deserted and lonely

   _____ b. unusual

   _____ c. bustling and cheerful

2. <u>Unscrupulous</u> con men simply pocketed people's fare and then disappeared.

   _____ a. talented

   _____ b. honest

   _____ c. deceitful

3. Smith was a gangster from Denver, Colorado, who brought his gang of 300 thugs up to prey upon <u>naive</u> stampeders.

   _____ a. suspicious

   _____ b. trusting and gullible

   _____ c. newly arrived

4. Smith's men robbed and shot prospectors <u>indiscriminately</u>.

   _____ a. showing careful thought

   _____ b. continually

   _____ c. randomly

5. Honest persons had no protection from the gang of rascals who plied their <u>nefarious</u> trade.

_____ a. popular

_____ b. evil

_____ c. good

_____ Score 3 points for each correct C answer.

_____ Score 2 points for each correct O answer.

_____ **Total Score:** Using Words Precisely

Enter the four total scores in the spaces below, and add them together to find your Reading Comprehension Score. Then record your score on the graph on page 197.

Score	Question Type	Lesson 17
_____	Finding the Main Idea	
_____	Recalling Facts	
_____	Making Inferences	
_____	Using Words Precisely	
_____	**Reading Comprehension Score**	

Author's Approach

Put an X in the box next to the correct answer.

1. The main purpose of the first paragraph is to
   ☐ a. explain how to pan for gold.
   ☐ b. describe the wildlife near Rabbit Creek.
   ☐ c. give the reader a clue about what will happen next.

2. What does the author imply by saying "Others died from a raging fever caused by eating the rotten meat of the dead horses"?
   ☐ a. Some stampeders did not pack enough food for the long trip to the Klondike.
   ☐ b. Some stampeders were fond of horse meat and were delighted to find some along the trail.
   ☐ c. Some stampeders purposely tried to poison their competitors by leaving rotten meat along the trail.

3. Choose the statement below that best describes the author's position in paragraph 8.
   ☐ a. Newspapers reported the news accurately.
   ☐ b. News articles and rumors exaggerated the amount of gold available in the Klondike.
   ☐ c. Newspaper reporters were to blame for criminal activity in the Klondike.

_____ Number of correct answers

Record your personal assessment of your work on the Critical Thinking Chart on page 198.

CRITICAL THINKING

Summarizing and Paraphrasing

Follow the directions provided for question 1. Put an X in the box next to the correct answer for question 2.

1. Reread paragraph 5 in the article. Below, write a summary of the paragraph in no more than 25 words.

_____

_____

_____

_____

Reread your summary and decide whether it covers the important ideas in the paragraph. Next, decide how to shorten the summary to 15 words or less without leaving out any essential information. Write this summary below.

_____

_____

_____

2. Choose the best one-sentence paraphrase for the following sentence from the article:

"Stampeders had their choice of several possible routes to the gold fields, each undesirable in its own way."

☐ a. Undesirable stampeders reached the gold fields in several ways.

☐ b. All the possible ways for stampeders to reach the gold fields had drawbacks.

☐ c. Stampeders chose one of several routes to reach the most desirable gold fields.

_____ Number of correct answers

Record your personal assessment of your work on the Critical Thinking Chart on page 198.

Critical Thinking

Put an X in the box next to the correct answer for questions 1, 2, and 3. Follow the directions provided for question 4.

1. From what the article told about the remoteness of the Klondike, you can predict that the area will

☐ a. lose its entire population within a few years.

☐ b. soon become the most populated area in North America.

☐ c. remain relatively empty for a long time.

2. What was the cause of the death of over 60 people who were using the Chilkoot Pass in the spring of 1898?

☐ a. starvation

☐ b. falls

☐ c. an avalanche

3. How is the Klondike gold rush related to the theme of this book?

☐ a. People from all walks of life found it exciting.

☐ b. It began with an amazing discovery.

☐ c. Many people made money as a result of the gold rush.

4. In which paragraph did you find your information or details to answer question 2?

_____

_____ Number of correct answers

Record your personal assessment of your work on the Critical Thinking Chart on page 198.

Self-Assessment

Before reading this article, I already knew

_____

_____

_____

Personal Response

I can't believe

_____

_____

_____

_____

LOUIS PASTEUR
Medical Wonder Worker

It is hard to imagine a more hideous way to die. The victims suffer from a brain-splitting fever. Dying of thirst, they beg for something to drink...but it's no use. They have lost their ability to swallow. Their jaws snap uncontrollably. There is no sleep, just endless tossing in agony. Only death, which is certain, brings relief from rabies.

2   For centuries, rabies was the scourge of the world. People contracted the disease after being bitten by a rabid dog or other animal. Each case was a little different. Some people who suffered through rabid animal attacks never got the disease. Those who did might show no symptoms for days or even weeks. Once the symptoms did appear, however, there was no hope of survival. The only chance most people had was to cauterize the wound before the disease took hold. That meant applying a red-hot poker to the animal bite as quickly as possible.

3   Then, in the 1880s, rabies met its match in a French scientist named Louis Pasteur. Born in 1822, his life was one

Before he developed the rabies vaccine, Louis Pasteur discovered that germs spread disease. As a result, doctors made sure their hands and instruments were clean before performing operations.

"I've got it!" moment after another. He was like a one-man scientific revolution. By the 1880's, his discoveries had already saved countless lives as well as whole industries. For example, his "germ theory" of disease led doctors to scrub their hands and instruments before they operated. That discovery alone saved hundreds of thousands of patients from needless infections.

4   Pasteur was the first to use heat to kill the bacteria that caused food and drink to spoil. The process he invented, known as "pasteurization," greatly benefited the milk, wine, and beer industries. Pasteur also saved the French silk industry. He did so by finding the germ that was killing silkworms. In addition, Pasteur discovered a way to cure anthrax and chicken cholera. Still, when he decided to take on rabies, some people wondered if he could work his magic again.

5   Pasteur knew that if he had any hope of discovering a vaccine for rabies, he had to go to the source. He would have to handle rabid dogs. Just getting close to these animals was an incredibly dangerous proposition. A rabid animal is out of its mind, and consequently will lash out at anyone near it. That was why so many people got rabies. Pasteur knew the risks, yet he was willing to take them.

6   In 1881, at the beginning of his research, all he knew for certain was that the disease was carried to humans in the saliva of rabid animals. He didn't have any idea what the rabies germ looked like. But Pasteur noticed that rabies took varying amounts of time to appear in victims. After puzzling over this fact, he suddenly thought of why this might be so. He figured that the germ had to travel from the bite mark to its ultimate destination, which Pasteur guessed was the victim's brain and spinal cord.

7   Sure enough, when Pasteur looked for the rabies germ inside the brains and spinal cords of dead victims, he found it. After identifying the germ, he was able to develop a vaccine against the disease. He made the vaccine from the minced spinal cord of rabid animals.

8   To test his vaccine, Pasteur placed a rabid bulldog in a cage with two healthy dogs. The mad bulldog instantly attacked the other dogs, biting them fiercely. Pasteur left one of the two dogs untreated. To the other he administered a series of shots containing his new vaccine. Every day for 14 days, Pasteur injected the vaccine into the dog, beginning with a very mild dose and slowly increasing the amount as the days passed.

9   As Pasteur predicted, the untreated dog went mad and died, while the treated dog remained healthy. "He has not evidenced one symptom of [rabies]," Pasteur wrote

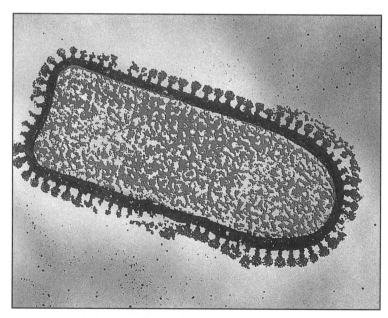

This electron microscope image shows rabies viruses invading a cell.

in 1885. "He is immune. The vaccine is a success."

10 That was exciting news, indeed; but would the vaccine prove effective on humans? Pasteur was reluctant to try it. After all, a few people who had been bitten by rabid animals had never contracted the disease. What if Pasteur inoculated such a person and gave him the disease instead of curing him? From Pasteur's perspective, that would be like murder. On the other hand, he couldn't wait until the symptoms appeared. Then it would be too late for the vaccine to do any good. Pasteur decided that there was only one thing for him to do: test the rabies vaccine on himself. He wouldn't tell anyone because people would certainly try to stop him.

11 As Pasteur made preparations for this drastic step, fate intervened. On July 6, 1886, a nine-year-old boy and his mother came to Louis Pasteur's office. The boy, Joseph Meister, had just been brutally attacked by a rabid dog on his way to school. The dog might have killed the defenseless boy right then and there if a man hadn't beaten the dog off with an iron bar. Still, the crazed animal had bitten Joseph more than a dozen times, leaving him so badly injured he could barely walk. But Joseph's mother wasn't focused on these wounds; all she could

think about was rabies. Fearful that Joseph would come down with the fatal disease, she rushed to see Pasteur. Could the scientist save her son?

12 Pasteur pointed out the grave risks involved. He explained that instead of saving her son, he might kill him. But the mother continued to plead with Pasteur, reminding him that if the boy had the disease he would surely die without Pasteur's help. Even if Pasteur wanted to try the vaccine on the boy, however, he couldn't do it alone because he wasn't a medical doctor. He needed the advice and consent of a physician. So he asked not one, but two doctors to examine Joseph. He hoped they could help him decide what course of action to take. After looking at the boy's wounds, the doctors agreed. In their opinion, the boy would get rabies. They urged Pasteur to use his vaccine—the sooner the better. Hearing their advice, Pasteur decided to go ahead and take the risk.

13 On the first day, Pasteur injected Joseph with a very mild form of the rabies germ. Each day, he gave the boy a slightly stronger dose. Throughout the 14-day treatment, Pasteur was a wreck. He couldn't sleep at night, half expecting to find Joseph foaming at the mouth each morning. But the boy stayed cheerful and healthy. On the 14th day, Pasteur injected

Joseph with a very powerful dose of rabies. Even then, the boy showed no signs of the disease.

14 Still, Pasteur had to wait and watch. Perhaps the rabies was just taking its time to reach the boy's spinal cord and brain. But as each day passed with no sign of disease in the boy, Pasteur's hopes rose. Joseph might live! Not only would that be a personal victory for Pasteur and the boy, but it would signal that the disease itself had been conquered. By August, Pasteur was finally convinced. "It has been 31 days since [Joseph] was bitten," he wrote in his notebook. "He is now quite safe. The vaccine is successful."

If you have been timed while reading this article, enter your reading time below. Then turn to the Words-per-Minute Table on page 195 and look up your reading speed (words per minute). Enter your reading speed on the graph on page 196.

Reading Time: Lesson 18

_____ : _____
Minutes   *Seconds*

A Finding the Main Idea

One statement below expresses the main idea of the article. One statement is too general, or too broad. The other statement explains only part of the article; it is too narrow. Label the statements using the following key:

M—Main Idea   **B—Too Broad**   **N—Too Narrow**

_____ 1. Louis Pasteur guessed that rabies germs travel from the bite mark to the victim's brain and spinal cord.

_____ 2. Louis Pasteur is credited with a number of important medical discoveries, including a vaccine to fight the dreadful disease of rabies.

_____ 3. The name of Louis Pasteur is well known in the history of medicine.

_____ Score 15 points for a correct M answer.

_____ Score 5 points for each correct B or N answer.

_____ **Total Score:** Finding the Main Idea

B Recalling Facts

How well do you remember the facts in the article? Put an X in the box next to the answer that correctly completes each statement about the article.

1. People contract rabies by
    ☐ a. being bitten by a rabid animal.
    ☐ b. eating food that contains the rabies germ.
    ☐ c. undergoing operations in which the doctor's hands are covered with the rabies germ.

2. To cauterize a wound means to
    ☐ a. wrap it with a clean bandage.
    ☐ b. wash it thoroughly.
    ☐ c. apply a red-hot poker to it.

3. All Pasteur knew for certain about rabies when he began his research was that
    ☐ a. it was carried to humans in the saliva of rabid animals.
    ☐ b. what the rabies germ looked like.
    ☐ c. the rabies germ always traveled to the brain or spinal cord of the victim.

4. Pasteur's rabies vaccine was made of
    ☐ a. contaminated milk.
    ☐ b. minced spinal cord from rabid animals.
    ☐ c. minced silkworms.

5. Pasteur observed Joseph Meister for
    ☐ a. 14 days.
    ☐ b. 31 days.
    ☐ c. one full year.

Score 5 points for each correct answer.

_____ **Total Score:** Recalling Facts

C | **Making Inferences**

When you combine your own experience and information from a text to draw a conclusion that is not directly stated in that text, you are making an inference. Below are five statements that may or may not be inferences based on information in the article. Label the statements using the following key:

C—Correct Inference   **F—Faulty Inference**

_____ 1. In the years since Pasteur's discovery of the rabies vaccine, no one has ever died of rabies.

_____ 2. Pasteur had many patients who came to him for medical treatment.

_____ 3. Louis Pasteur had tremendous curiosity and perseverance.

_____ 4. Pasteur believed that the life of a dog was of less importance than a human life.

_____ 5. Louis Pasteur cared a great deal about the welfare of Joseph Meister.

Score 5 points for each correct answer.

_____ **Total Score:** Making Inferences

D | **Using Words Precisely**

Each numbered sentence below contains an underlined word or phrase from the article. Following the sentence are three definitions. One definition is closest to the meaning of the underlined word. One definition is opposite or nearly opposite. Label those two definitions using the following key. Do not label the remaining definition.

C—Closest   **O—Opposite or Nearly Opposite**

1. It is hard to imagine a more <u>hideous</u> way to die.

_____ a. expensive

_____ b. horrible, disgusting

_____ c. pleasant

2. He made the vaccine from the <u>minced</u> spinal cord of rabid animals.

_____ a. infected

_____ b. whole

_____ c. cut up into tiny pieces

3. "He has not <u>evidenced</u> one symptom of [rabies]...."

_____ a. hidden

_____ b. welcomed

_____ c. shown

4. Pasteur was <u>reluctant</u> to try it.

_____ a. hesitant

_____ b. eager

_____ c. the first

5. As Pasteur made preparations for this <u>drastic</u> step, fate intervened.

_____ a. extreme, desperate

_____ b. unexpected

_____ c. cautious

_____ Score 3 points for each correct C answer.

_____ Score 2 points for each correct O answer.

_____ **Total Score:** Using Words Precisely

Enter the four total scores in the spaces below, and add them together to find your Reading Comprehension Score. Then record your score on the graph on page 197.

Score	Question Type	Lesson 18
_____	Finding the Main Idea	
_____	Recalling Facts	
_____	Making Inferences	
_____	Using Words Precisely	
_____	**Reading Comprehension Score**	

Author's Approach

Put an X in the box next to the correct answer.

1. The main purpose of the first paragraph is to
☐ a. create a tense mood.
☐ b. explain how Louis Pasteur conquered rabies.
☐ c. describe the symptoms of rabies.

2. What is the author's purpose in writing "Louis Pasteur: Medical Wonder Worker"?
☐ a. To encourage the reader to become a medical researcher
☐ b. To inform the reader about the contributions of Louis Pasteur
☐ c. To emphasize the similarities between rabies and smallpox

3. From the statements below, choose those that you believe the author would agree with.
☐ a. Rabies is a horrible, frightening disease.
☐ b. We all owe Louis Pasteur a debt of gratitude.
☐ c. Louis Pasteur could not stick with a project up to its completion.

4. In this article, "As Pasteur made preparations for this drastic step [testing the vaccine on himself], fate intervened" means
☐ a. Something unexpectedly stopped Pasteur from testing the vaccine on himself.
☐ b. An unexpected event caused Pasteur to speed up his plans to test the vaccine on himself.
☐ c. Pasteur was willing to delay his test for almost any reason because he was afraid.

_____ Number of correct answers

Record your personal assessment of your work on the Critical Thinking Chart on page 198.

Summarizing and Paraphrasing

Follow the directions provided for question 1. Put an X in the box next to the correct answer for question 2.

1. Look for the important ideas and events in paragraphs 6 and 7. Summarize those paragraphs in one or two sentences.

_____

_____

_____

2. Below are summaries of the article. Choose the summary that says all the most important things about the article but in the fewest words.

☐ a. One of Louis Pasteur's greatest discoveries was the vaccine for rabies. He made it by mincing the spinal cord of rabid animals. The first human to test the vaccine was a boy who had been bitten repeatedly by a rabid dog. The boy's frantic mother insisted that Pasteur try his new vaccine on her son. After treating the boy and observing him for a month, Pasteur declared the vaccine successful.

☐ b. Louis Pasteur tested his new rabies vaccine on a nine-year-old boy who had been bitten by a rabid dog. After a month of treatment and observation, Pasteur claimed success for the vaccine made from minced spinal cords of rabid animals.

☐ c. Louis Pasteur was known for many discoveries; one of his greatest discoveries is the process known as "pasteurization."

_____ Number of correct answers

Record your personal assessment of your work on the Critical Thinking Chart on page 198.

Critical Thinking

Put an X in the box next to the correct answer for questions 1, 2, 4, and 5. Follow the directions provided for question 3.

1. Which of the following statements from the article is an opinion rather than a fact?

☐ a. "On the 14th day, Pasteur injected Joseph with a very powerful dose of rabies."

☐ b. "Pasteur was the first to use heat to kill the bacteria that caused food and drink to spoil."

☐ c. "It is hard to imagine a more hideous way to die."

2. From what the article told about Joseph Meister's condition after treatment, you can infer that

☐ a. Louis Pasteur was dismayed with the outcome of treatment.

☐ b. the doctors were sorry they had advised Pasteur to treat the boy.

☐ c. his mother was glad that she had pleaded with Pasteur to treat him.

3. Choose from the letters below to correctly complete the following statement. Write the letters on the lines.

On the positive side, _____, but on the negative side _____.

a. one untreated dog went mad and died

b. Pasteur learned a lot by testing his new vaccine on dogs

c. Pasteur injected his new vaccine into one dog as part of a test

4. What was the cause of the variance in times that rabies took to kill its victims?

☐ a. Some victims were stronger than others.

☐ b. There were many different kinds of rabies germs.

☐ c. The rabies germ took different times to reach the victim's brain and spinal cord.

5. What did you have to do to answer question 4?

☐ a. find a comparison (how things are the same)

☐ b. find a list (a number of things)

☐ c. find a cause (why something happened)

_____ Number of correct answers

Record your personal assessment of your work on the Critical Thinking Chart on page 198.

Personal Response

What would you have done if you had been Pasteur, and Joseph Meister's mother asked you to test the vaccine on her son?

_____

_____

_____

Self-Assessment

I can't really understand how

_____

_____

_____

_____

THE SEARCH FOR ANCIENT ANCESTORS

Mary Leakey is shown here at the end of the trail of hominid (human) footprints preserved in volcanic ash. This trail was discovered in Tanzania in 1978.

Even archaeologists need a little fun once in a while. So after a hot dusty day under the African sun digging for fossils in Laetoli, Tanzania, Dr. Andrew Hill and a few of his colleagues were in the mood for a snowball fight. Since there wasn't any snow, however, they began pelting each other with large clumps of dried elephant dung. "Then, as is so often the case in pivotal discoveries," wrote team leader Mary Leakey, "luck intervened." Someone heaved a piece of dung at Hill's head. As he ducked to avoid the missile, he noticed a series of punctures in the ground.

2   These marks turned out to be animal footprints. But they weren't just any animal prints; they came from the distant past—roughly 3.7 million years ago. And they led to one of the greatest finds ever in the field of archaeology.

3   The prints had been made when animals walked over ground that was covered with new volcanic ash and moistened by a light rain. As the ash hardened, the gooey ground turned to concrete. Over many, many years the

footprints were covered by dust, dirt, and more ash. Perhaps as much as 70 feet of debris once covered these prints. Later, weathering and erosion washed away almost all the covering, exposing the footprints once again.

4   Team leader Mary Leakey was excited by the prints. She knew that if animal prints had been preserved in this area, perhaps there were human prints, too. She didn't expect to find anything as old as the animal prints; no one thought humans were walking around more than 3 million years ago. Still, she hoped to find some evidence of human ancestors.

5   For two years Leakey searched. At last, in 1978, she and her research team noticed what they thought were hominid (human-like) footprints. On August 2, Mary spent three hours carefully examining one of the clearer footprints with a dental pick and a small brush. She saw that it had a heel, toes, and arch. There was no mistaking it; this was the print of an early human. "Now this," Mary said, "really is something to put on the mantelpiece."

6   Amazingly, the print Leakey examined was over three and a half million years old. It was part of a trail of prints stretching 75 feet across the plain. The prints were made by two human-like creatures who "walked fully upright with a bipedal (two-legged), free-striding gait." These footprints showed that our human ancestors walked on two feet much earlier than anyone had previously thought.

7   By studying the trail of prints, Mary was able to reconstruct what the walkers may have experienced as they hiked across Laetoli. At one point, the smaller of the two, probably a female, stopped and paused. Then, Leakey speculated, she "turn[ed] to the left to glance at some possible threat…. This motion, so intensely human, transcends time. Three million six hundred thousand years ago, a remote ancestor—just as you or I—experienced a moment of doubt."

8   For Mary Leakey, this was a moment of glory. But although the Laetoli prints were her greatest discovery, they were not her only claim to fame. Leakey had a number of successes during the many years she spent in the dry valleys of East Africa.

9   As a young girl growing up in France and England, Mary had two passions—art and archaeology. "I dug things up," she said. "I was curious, and then I liked to draw what I found….The first money I ever earned was for drawing stone tools."

10   Her formal schooling ended early, when she was expelled from school for setting off an explosion in her chemistry class. She continued to draw, however, and when she was 20, her illustrations

Mary Leakey and her husband Louis examine skull pieces found in Tanganyika in 1959.

caught the eye of Louis Leakey, a famed archaeologist. He wanted her to help him with drawings for a book. Mary agreed, and before long a romance ensued. In 1936, the couple married and moved to Africa. There, in time, they would became the most famous archaeological team in the world.

11 Among Mary's accomplishments was the 1948 discovery of a fossilized ape skull. It belonged to a tiny 16-million-year-old ape the Leakeys called Proconsul. No one had ever found such a skull before.

12 In July 1959, Mary made another spectacular discovery. While Louis lay in his tent ill with influenza, Mary went out into the hot sun as usual. She worked on her hands and knees, brushing away dirt from the floor of Olduvai Gorge. On this day she got lucky. She spotted some teeth and part of a jaw lying amidst the dust. She rushed back to her husband, shouting, "I've found him—found our man!" And indeed she had. The remains turned out to be part of an ancient skull belong-

ing to a hominid later named "nutcracker man" because of his huge jaw and teeth. This skull was dated at 1.8 million years, making it the oldest human ancestor found up to that point.

13 Although Mary did most of the actual work, Louis Leakey was the one who got most of the applause. "For many decades, Louis was given the credit, because that's the way the world looked at science, as a man's field," said fellow archaeologist Richard Potts. "But Mary was the one who did the work. Mary was the real scientist in the family."

14 The truth became clear after Louis Leakey died in 1972. Mary had always been shy and reluctant to maintain a public profile. Louis was the one who publicized their work. With him gone, however, Mary had no choice. Now she was the one who had to give speeches, attend conferences, and seek financing. As she did so, she at last began to receive the professional recognition she deserved. In time several major universities awarded

her honorary degrees for her pioneer work in archaeology.

15 After her death in 1996, Dr. Alan Walker summed up Mary Leakey's life. "She was one of the world's great originals," he said. "Untrained except in art, she developed techniques of excavation and descriptive archaeology and did it all on her own in the middle of Africa. It was an extraordinary life." 🖋

If you have been timed while reading this article, enter your reading time below. Then turn to the Words-per-Minute Table on page 195 and look up your reading speed (words per minute). Enter your reading speed on the graph on page 196.

Reading Time: Lesson 19

_____ : _____
Minutes   Seconds

A Finding the Main Idea

One statement below expresses the main idea of the article. One statement is too general, or too broad. The other statement explains only part of the article; it is too narrow. Label the statements using the following key:

M—Main Idea   **B—Too Broad**   **N—Too Narrow**

_____ 1. It is only through persistent research that humans can learn about their distant past.

_____ 2. Mary Leakey, along with her husband, Louis, spent her life searching for and finding evidence of human ancestors.

_____ 3. Although Mary Leakey did most of the work, her husband, Louis Leakey, was given most of the credit.

_____ Score 15 points for a correct M answer.

_____ Score 5 points for each correct B or N answer.

_____ **Total Score:** Finding the Main Idea

B Recalling Facts

How well do you remember the facts in the article? Put an X in the box next to the answer that correctly completes each statement about the article.

1. Mary Leakey found ancient human-like footprints in
   ☐ a. France.
   ☐ b. Tanzania.
   ☐ c. England.

2. When a member of Mary Leakey's team found footprints of animals in hardened volcanic ash, Mary
   ☐ a. had her moment of greatest glory.
   ☐ b. knew for sure that humans had walked on two legs earlier than others had guessed.
   ☐ c. hoped that she would find human footprints nearby.

3. In 1948, the Leakeys found the skull of an ancient ape they called
   ☐ a. Proconsul.
   ☐ b. Olduvai Gorge.
   ☐ c. nutcracker man.

4. After Louis Leakey died, Mary
   ☐ a. had to seek financing.
   ☐ b. gave up her archaeological research.
   ☐ c. went back to school.

5. Mary didn't like to give speeches because she
   ☐ a. was shy.
   ☐ b. had no formal training.
   ☐ c. had nothing original to say.

Score 5 points for each correct answer.

_____ **Total Score:** Recalling Facts

C | Making Inferences

When you combine your own experience and information from a text to draw a conclusion that is not directly stated in that text, you are making an inference. Below are five statements that may or may not be inferences based on information in the article. Label the statements using the following key:

C—Correct Inference   **F—Faulty Inference**

_____ 1. Mary Leakey probably would have become an archaeologist even if she had never met Louis Leakey.

_____ 2. To be an archaeologist, you need patience and attention to detail.

_____ 3. Mary Leakey could not sustain her interest in archaeology for very long.

_____ 4. The Leakeys were careful and thorough when they presented their findings to other science experts.

_____ 5. Mary Leakey always enjoyed drawing fossils more than she liked looking for them.

Score 5 points for each correct answer.

_____ **Total Score:** Making Inferences

D | Using Words Precisely

Each numbered sentence below contains an underlined word or phrase from the article. Following the sentence are three definitions. One definition is closest to the meaning of the underlined word. One definition is opposite or nearly opposite. Label those two definitions using the following key. Do not label the remaining definition.

C—Closest   **O—Opposite or Nearly Opposite**

1. "Then, as is so often the case in <u>pivotal</u> discoveries," wrote team leader Mary Leakey, "luck intervened."

_____ a. essential

_____ b. trivial

_____ c. new

2. Someone <u>heaved</u> a piece of dung at Hill's head.

_____ a. aimed

_____ b. caught

_____ c. threw

3. The prints had been made when animals walked over ground that was…<u>moistened</u> by a light rain.

_____ a. made slightly wet

_____ b. blown away

_____ c. dried out

4. By studying the trail of prints, Mary was able to <u>reconstruct</u> what the walkers may have experienced as they hiked across Laetoli.

_____ a. unable to imagine

_____ b. build again in one's mind

_____ c. ignore

5. Mary agreed, and before long a romance <u>ensued</u>.

_____ a. happened beforehand
_____ b. followed
_____ c. was made public

_____ Score 3 points for each correct C answer.
_____ Score 2 points for each correct O answer.
_____ **Total Score:** Using Words Precisely

Enter the four total scores in the spaces below, and add them together to find your Reading Comprehension Score. Then record your score on the graph on page 197.

Score	Question Type	Lesson 19
____	Finding the Main Idea	
____	Recalling Facts	
____	Making Inferences	
____	Using Words Precisely	
____	**Reading Comprehension Score**	

Author's Approach

Put an X in the box next to the correct answer.

1. Which of the following statements from the article best describes Mary Leakey?
☐ a. "In July 1959, Mary made another spectacular discovery."
☐ b. "'But Mary was the one who did the work. Mary was the real scientist in the family.'"
☐ c. "Among Mary's accomplishments was the 1948 discovery of a fossilized ape skull."

2. Judging by statements from the article "The Search for Ancient Ancestors," you can conclude that the author wants the reader to think that
☐ a. Louis Leakey doesn't deserve any credit for the couple's discoveries.
☐ b. Mary and Louis Leakey worked well together.
☐ c. Mary Leakey always wanted to be in the spotlight, but Louis wouldn't let her give speeches.

3. How is the author's purpose for writing the article expressed in paragraph 8?
☐ a. The author points out that Mary Leakey spent many years in Africa.
☐ b. The author argues that the Laetoli prints were Mary Leakey's greatest discovery.
☐ c. The author points out that Mary Leakey was a successful archaeologist for many years.

CRITICAL THINKING

4. The author tells this story mainly by

☐ a. comparing different topics.

☐ b. using his or her imagination and creativity.

☐ c. telling different stories about the same person.

_____ Number of correct answers

Record your personal assessment of your work on the Critical Thinking Chart on page 198.

Summarizing and Paraphrasing

Follow the directions provided for question 1. Put an X in the box next to the correct answer for question 2.

1. Reread paragraph 11 in the article. Below, write a summary of the paragraph in no more than 25 words.

_____

_____

_____

Reread your summary and decide whether it covers the important ideas in the paragraph. Next, decide how to shorten the summary to 15 words or less without leaving out any essential information. Write this summary below.

_____

_____

2. Read the statement about the article below. Then read the paraphrase of that statement. Choose the reason that best tells why the paraphrase does not say the same thing as the statement.

Statement: Animals had stepped into wet volcanic ash, and then the ground around their footprints dried out and hardened.

Paraphrase: The ground which had been moist soon dried out and hardened.

☐ a. Paraphrase says too much.

☐ b. Paraphrase doesn't say enough.

☐ c. Paraphrase doesn't agree with the statement about the article.

_____ Number of correct answers

Record your personal assessment of your work on the Critical Thinking Chart on page 198.

Critical Thinking

Put an X in the box next to the correct answer for questions 1, 2, and 4. Follow the directions provided for question 3.

1. Which of the following statements from the article is an opinion rather than a fact?

☐ a. "While Louis lay in his tent ill with influenza, Mary went out into the hot sun as usual."

☐ b. "As a young girl growing up in France and England, Mary had two passions—art and archaeology."

☐ c. "'She [Mary Leakey] was one of the world's great originals.'"

CRITICAL THINKING

2. Judging by the events in the article, you can predict that the following will happen next:

☐ a. archaeologists will continue to discover more about the human past.

☐ b. archaeologists will stop trying to find out more about the distant human past because everything is now known.

☐ c. archaeologists will decide that the Leakeys' discoveries are inaccurate and worthless.

3. Think about cause-effect relationships in the article. Fill in the blanks in the cause-effect chart, drawing from the letters below.

Cause	Effect
Animals walked in wet volcanic ash.	_____
Mary Leakey set off an explosion in class.	_____
_____	Louis Leakey usually spoke for both Mary and himself.

a. Mary Leakey was shy.

b. Mary Leakey was expelled from school.

c. Their footprints remained when the ground hardened.

4. If you were an archaeologist, how could you use the information in the article to make discoveries?

☐ a. Like the Leakeys, maintain your enthusiasm and work hard.

☐ b. Like Mary Leakey, draw pictures of everything you find.

☐ c. Like the Leakeys, look only in Africa.

_____ Number of correct answers

Record your personal assessment of your work on the Critical Thinking Chart on page 198.

Personal Response

I know the feeling that Mary Leakey had when she wasn't given credit for her work because

_____

_____

_____

_____

Self-Assessment

When reading the article, I was having trouble with

_____

_____

_____

_____

CRITICAL THINKING

FINDING THE TITANIC

At 11:40 P.M. on April 14, 1912, the White Star ocean liner *Titanic* hit an iceberg about 400 miles from Newfoundland, Canada. In less than three hours, the "unsinkable" ship slipped beneath the waves of the frigid Atlantic, taking 1,513 people with it. This tragedy became what many people believe to be the most riveting ocean drama of all time. It has served as the subject of songs, poetry, books, and movies.

2   There have, of course, been many other disasters at sea. But the *Titanic* seems to hold a unique spot in people's hearts. The liner was the largest passenger ship in the world. It was the fastest and best-equipped vessel of its day. The *Titanic* was making its maiden voyage, and was carrying some of the richest people in the world. So the ship had plenty of attention even before it struck the iceberg. When it sank, the *Titanic* made headlines around the world.

3   The ship had hardly settled on the ocean floor before people began hatching plans to salvage the fortune in jewels and cash the *Titanic* supposedly had on board. No scheme, it seemed, was too harebrained. Englishman Doug Wooley had a couple of

The promenade deck of the Titanic *as it appeared in 1912. Inset (lower left): The remains of the* Titanic's *promenade deck at the bottom of the Atlantic Ocean.*

off-the-wall ideas. One was to use liquid nitrogen to freeze the ship into a giant block of ice. Then the *Titanic* would simply float up to the surface. Another was to fill the *Titanic*'s hull with millions of buoyant ping-pong balls. That, too, would cause the *Titanic* to bob to the surface.

4   Wooley never got to try either of these schemes because he never found the *Titanic*. And for a long time neither did anyone else. The stormy and unpredictable North Atlantic made searching for the ship nearly impossible. Also, the *Titanic* went down in more than two and a half miles of water. So for 73 years, the ocean kept the site of the ship's watery grave a secret.

5   It would take the most sophisticated equipment of the late 20th century to find and explore the *Titanic*'s remains. During the 1980s, the U.S. Navy developed an unmanned sonar and video sub. The Navy could have just lowered it off the side of a boat in the middle of the sea and turned it on to see what they could see. But Dr. Robert Ballard of the Woods Hole Oceanographic Institute had a better idea for testing the

new sub. He wanted to use it to search for a known object—the *Titanic*. Navy officials agreed to the plan. So in 1985, Ballard and his crew, along with a team of French explorers, began scanning for the ocean floor for the *Titanic*.

6   Even with the best equipment, it was not easy to locate the sunken vessel. The explorers had a rough idea where the ship went down but no one knew the precise coordinates. That meant the Americans and French would have to search many square miles of open ocean.

The Titanic *leaves Southampton, England, on its maiden voyage, April 1912.*

7   The French began to search a 150-square-mile section in late June with their own sonar device. They searched about 80% of the target area with no success. Then Ballard arrived in August aboard the U.S. Navy research vessel *Knorr*. He began sweeping the remaining 20% by trolling with the navy sonar sub at 12,500 feet.

8   On the morning of September 1, Ballard had just left his post in the command center to take a nap. Suddenly, the ship's cook burst into his room to wake him. "The guys in the [control center] think you should come down," he announced. Ballard pulled on some clothes over his pajamas and rushed to the control center. As soon as he saw the video image of a boiler, Ballard knew the search for the *Titanic* was over. "That's it!" he shouted.

9   "We went smack-dang over a gorgeous boiler," Ballard later said. "It was just bang, there we were on top of [the *Titanic*.]"

10   Many of the people who died on the *Titanic* did so because there were not enough lifeboats for everyone. As Ballard's group looked at images of the sunken ship, they got a chilling reminder of what happened the night of April 14, 1912. "[There were] empty lifeboat davits hanging there," recalled Ballard. "That's the last thing many of the people saw as they were looking for a lifeboat."

11   So, after celebrating their victory, Ballard's crew turned more somber. What they had found was not only a ship but a tomb for 1,513 people. Ballard organized a brief memorial service for all these who

had died. Later, he vehemently opposed any efforts to raise the *Titanic*. "There is no light at that depth, and little life can be found," he said. "It is a quiet, peaceful place and a fitting place for the remains of this greatest of sea tragedies to rest. Forever may it remain that way. And may God bless those now-found souls."

12   For a while, Ballard kept the exact coordinates a secret. He didn't want greedy treasure hunters desecrating the tomb of the *Titanic*. He and his crew returned to the site the following summer to do a thorough exploration of the ship. This time Ballard used a manned sub called *Alvin* to see the ship up close. It took Alvin two and a half hours just to dive deep enough to reach the *Titanic*. When Ballard, traveling in *Alvin*, approached the ship, the sight shook him. "You really felt it when you were there, the sheer carnage," he said. "It looked violent and destructive."

13   Ballard's explorations answered many questions about the last hours of the ship. Did the ship, as some eyewitnesses had claimed, break in half? The answer was yes. Ballard found the bow of the *Titanic* in good shape sitting upright on the bottom of the ocean. The mangled stern, however, was found some 1,800 feet away with tons of debris scattered all around. Ballard believed that the water-filled bow raised the ship's stern out of the water, causing it to break off just before it sank.

14   Ballard found "absolutely no evidence" of a 300-foot gash along the side of the ship. Most people had believed initial

reports that the iceberg had ripped a long hole along the side of the *Titanic*. Instead, Ballard believed that the iceberg hit the liner in such a way as to buckle the hull and pop the rivets.

15   In 11 dives, Robert Ballard photographed the *Titanic* from all angles. Using a remote-controlled robot named J.J., he also explored the inside of the massive ship. The robot took thousands of photos of the bow, stern, deck, grand staircase, chandeliers, and even a coffee cup that was in perfect shape. Said Ballard, "There is not a square inch of the *Titanic* that has not been photographed in beautiful detail."

16   Ballard found no human remains, however. Sea organisms had long since eaten all such organic matter as well as wooden railings and leather suitcases. "The only thing that even looked human," Ballard said, "was a little doll's head." 🍃

If you have been timed while reading this article, enter your reading time below. Then turn to the Words-per-Minute Table on page 195 and look up your reading speed (words per minute). Enter your reading speed on the graph on page 196.

Reading Time: Lesson 20

_____ : _____
Minutes   *Seconds*

A | Finding the Main Idea

One statement below expresses the main idea of the article. One statement is too general, or too broad. The other statement explains only part of the article; it is too narrow. Label the statements using the following key:

M—Main Idea   **B—Too Broad**   **N—Too Narrow**

_____ 1. The *Titanic* has inspired romantics and treasure hunters ever since its plunge to the bottom of the ocean in 1912.

_____ 2. Robert Ballard feels that the *Titanic* should be allowed to rest in peace.

_____ 3. Other attempts to find the *Titanic* had failed, but in 1985 Robert Ballard found the sunken ship and photographed it in detail.

_____ Score 15 points for a correct M answer.

_____ Score 5 points for each correct B or N answer.

_____ **Total Score:** Finding the Main Idea

B | Recalling Facts

How well do you remember the facts in the article? Put an X in the box next to the answer that correctly completes each statement about the article.

1. The *Titanic* sank after it

☐ a. suffered an explosion that ripped apart its hull.

☐ b. ran aground.

☐ c. hit an iceberg.

2. The *Titanic* remained untouched for

☐ a. 26 years.

☐ b. 73 years.

☐ c. 92 years.

3. The unmanned sonar and video sub was developed by the

☐ a. U.S. Navy.

☐ b. U.S. Army.

☐ c. U.S. Marines.

4. The manned sub that Ballard used to photograph the *Titanic* was called

☐ a. *Alvin.*

☐ b. *J.J.*

☐ c. *Knorr.*

5. Ballard's photos verified that the *Titanic*

☐ a. suffered a 300-foot rip in its side.

☐ b. broke in half.

☐ c. really did have enough lifeboats for everyone.

Score 5 points for each correct answer.

_____ **Total Score:** Recalling Facts

C   Making Inferences

When you combine your own experience and information from a text to draw a conclusion that is not directly stated in that text, you are making an inference. Below are five statements that may or may not be inferences based on information in the article. Label the statements using the following key:

C—Correct Inference   F—Faulty Inference

_____   1. The captain of the *Titanic* was not expecting to see icebergs at that time of year.

_____   2. Navy officials trusted Robert Ballard to take good care of their sub.

_____   3. French researchers had no real interest in the *Titanic*; they were simply curious about how well the video sub worked.

_____   4. Ballard found many other sunken ships when he searched the ocean bottom with the sonar sub.

_____   5. Ballard feels sympathy for the people who died on the *Titanic*.

Score 5 points for each correct answer.

_____ **Total Score:** Making Inferences

D   Using Words Precisely

Each numbered sentence below contains an underlined word or phrase from the article. Following the sentence are three definitions. One definition is closest to the meaning of the underlined word. One definition is opposite or nearly opposite. Label those two definitions using the following key. Do not label the remaining definition.

C—Closest   O—Opposite or Nearly Opposite

1. The ship had hardly settled on the ocean floor before people began hatching plans to <u>salvage</u> the fortune in jewels and cash the *Titanic* supposedly had on board..

_____   a. retrieve or get back

_____   b. view

_____   c. abandon

2. No scheme, it seemed, was too <u>harebrained</u>.

_____   a. cheap

_____   b. silly

_____   c. sensible

3. Another was to fill the *Titanic*'s hull with millions of <u>buoyant</u> ping-pong balls.

_____   a. white

_____   b. tending to sink

_____   c. capable of floating

4. He didn't want greedy treasure hunters <u>desecrating</u> the tomb of the *Titanic*.

_____ a. respecting

_____ b. dishonoring

_____ c. entering

5. The <u>mangled</u> stern, however, was found some 1,800 feet away with tons of debris scattered all around.

_____ a. perfect

_____ b. huge

_____ c. damaged

_____ Score 3 points for each correct C answer.

_____ Score 2 points for each correct O answer.

_____ **Total Score:** Using Words Precisely

Enter the four total scores in the spaces below, and add them together to find your Reading Comprehension Score. Then record your score on the graph on page 197.

Score	Question Type	Lesson 20
_____	Finding the Main Idea	
_____	Recalling Facts	
_____	Making Inferences	
_____	Using Words Precisely	
_____	**Reading Comprehension Score**	

Author's Approach

Put an X in the box next to the correct answer.

1. The author uses the first sentence of the article to

☐ a. inform the reader about the general topic of the article.

☐ b. describe springtime in the North Atlantic.

☐ c. compare the *Titanic* with other ships.

2. Judging by statements from the article "Finding the *Titanic*," you can conclude that the author wants the reader to think that

☐ a. Ballard was right when he recommended that the *Titanic* be allowed to remain untouched.

☐ b. Ballard had no right to keep the remains of the *Titanic* off limits to treasure hunters.

☐ c. it is impossible to keep treasure hunters from raiding the *Titanic*.

3. What does the author imply by the statement "In less than three hours, the 'unsinkable' ship slipped beneath the waves of the frigid Atlantic, taking 1,513 people with it"?

☐ a. The Atlantic was particularly cold that year.

☐ b. People who thought the *Titanic* was unsinkable were wrong.

☐ c. The *Titanic* took a long time to finally sink.

_____ Number of correct answers

Record your personal assessment of your work on the Critical Thinking Chart on page 198.

Summarizing and Paraphrasing

Put an X in the box next to the correct answer.

1. Complete the following one-sentence summary of the article using the lettered phrases from the phrase bank below. Write the letters on the lines.

> **Phrase Bank:**
>
> a. Ballard's assertion that there are no human remains on the ship
>
> b. a description of the sinking of the *Titanic*
>
> c. how Robert Ballard found and photographed the ship

The article about "Finding the *Titanic*" begins with _____, goes on to explain _____, and ends with _____.

2. Choose the sentence that correctly restates the following sentence from the article:

"Ballard believed that the water-filled bow raised the ship's stern out of the water, causing it to break off just before it sank."

☐ a. Ballard maintained that the bow broke off just before the water-filled stern sank.

☐ b. Ballard believed that when the ship's stern filled with water, it raised the bow out of the water until it broke off.

☐ c. In Ballard's opinion, the sinking of the bow made the stern rise out of the water and snap off before it, too, sank.

> _____ Number of correct answers
>
> Record your personal assessment of your work on the Critical Thinking Chart on page 198.

Critical Thinking

Follow the directions provided for questions 1 and 2. Put an X in the box next to the correct answer for the other questions.

1. For each statement below, write O if it expresses an opinion or write F if it expresses a fact.

_____ a. People should remember and learn from the tragedy of the *Titanic*.

_____ b. Ballard organized a memorial service for the passengers who went down with the *Titanic*.

_____ c. A remote-controlled robot took detailed photographs of the interior of the *Titanic*.

2. Read paragraph 1. Then choose from the letters below to correctly complete the following statement. Write the letters on the lines.

According to paragraph 1, _____ because _____.

a. the *Titanic* was about 400 miles from Newfoundland.

b. the *Titanic* sank

c. the ship hit an iceberg

3. How is "Finding the *Titanic*" related to the theme of this book?

☐ a. This article tells the story of the locating of a ship that many people find fascinating.

☐ b. This article tells of the tragedy of the *Titanic*'s sinking.

☐ c. This article compares the sinking of the *Titanic* with that of other ships.

4. What did you have to do to answer question 2?

☐ a. find an effect (something that happened)

☐ b. find a description (how something looks)

☐ c. find a comparison (how things are the same)

_____ Number of correct answers

Record your personal assessment of your work on the Critical Thinking Chart on page 198.

Before reading this article, I already knew

_____

_____

_____

_____

Personal Response

I disagree with the author because

_____

_____

_____

_____

STUDYING THE SECRET LIVES OF ORANGUTANS

Birute Galdikas spent years studying orangutans. Here she is seen with one of these primates.

It had been raining for hours. Hunched in their small dugout canoe, Birute Galdikas and her husband, Rod Brindamour, were drenched to the bone. For six hours they had been paddling along this muddy river in the rainforest of southern Borneo. Birute squinted through the rain, looking for some sign that they had reached the abandoned park ranger station that was to be their campsite. All she could see, however, were crocodiles lining the banks of the river and deadly snakes hanging from the tangled vines that covered the tree branches.

2   Birute had never been into the jungle before. She had become interested in anthropology while growing up in Canada. But until now, everything she knew about the field had come from books. In 1969, the 23-year-old Birute had heard a lecture by the famous anthropologist, Louis Leakey. Leakey believed people could learn a great deal about early humans by watching modern-day apes. He had already sent two women out to study wild apes. Jane Goodall was in Africa observing chimps. Dian Fossey was

studying mountain gorillas in another part of Africa.

3 According to Leakey, there was a third group of apes that should be studied. That group was the orangutans, which could be found only on the Indonesian islands of Borneo and Sumatra. Excited by Dr. Leakey's talk, Birute volunteered for the job. In the fall of 1971, she and her husband filled their backpacks with food, clothes, flashlights, a camera, and a book on the snakes of Asia. They headed off for Borneo. Now, as they struggled up the Sekonyer River, her husband wondered if they had made a big mistake.

4 Rod's misgivings were heightened when they finally arrived at the thatched-roof hut in Kalimantan that was to be their home. "It was filthy and filled with all sorts of vermin," Birute recalled. "Rod later told me he fully expected me to turn around and demand to be taken back." Birute herself had no such thoughts. She later reported, "I felt, when I came to Kalimantan, I was coming home."

5 As Rod worked to clean the hut and cut trails through the surrounding jungle, Birute set out in search of orangutans. She wasn't sure exactly how to locate them. Before coming to Borneo, she had met with Jane Goodall, hoping to get some ideas. "What am I going to do when I get to the field?" she had asked Goodall nervously. "You're going to do exactly what I did," answered Goodall, "You're going to go out and find them."

6 It wasn't as easy as it sounded. Orangutans are solitary creatures. They do not live in groups, nor do they socialize the way other apes do. In addition, they are arboreal, meaning they live primarily in the trees. They spend most of their time in the canopy of the rainforest, some 20 or 30 feet in the air. From time to time, Birute did spot an orangutan or two high in the trees. She tried her best to follow them, but they always seemed to slip away from her before the end of the day.

7 Birute soon became exhausted from the effort of pushing her way through the thick undergrowth and slogging through huge swamps. "I'd get up for days in a row at 3:30 A.M., walk through those swamps, wet up to my waist, mosquitoes biting me at every turn, leeches leeching me," she reported. "It was grueling physical and mental punishment." By sunset, she added, the leeches would be "bloated with [my] blood." They "fell out of [my] socks, dropped off [my] neck, and even squirmed out of [my] underwear."

8 Eventually Birute developed ulcerous sores on her legs, the result of spending so much time in the black swamp water. She also suffered severe skin burns after sitting down on a log that oozed toxic sap. Then, too, there were the tropical diseases. Birute caught malaria, a disease that would plague her for years to come. She also came down with dengue fever, a disease she describes as causing "pain so bad you know why people kill themselves to end it."

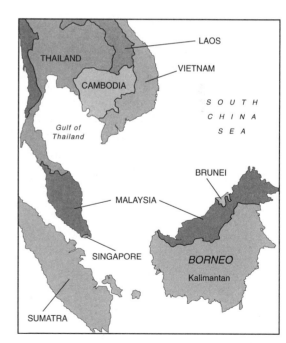

Kalimantan, part of the island of Borneo, where Galdikas went to study orangutans

9 Still, she declares, she never considered giving up. "I was born to do this," she says simply. And it time, her patience and perseverance paid off. Shortly before Christmas, she managed to follow a mother and baby orangutan all day, even witnessing the mother build a nest in the trees and bed down with her baby for the night. Very early the next morning, Birute returned to the spot and found—to her delight—the animals were still there. "It was the best Christmas present I ever had," she said. "The breakthrough was that we knew we could follow them until evening, then find them in the same tree the next day."

10 From then on, there was no stopping Birute. She doggedly followed orangutans through miles of dense jungle. At one point, she stayed with a mother and baby for 100 straight days. She compiled book after book of records detailing the behavior of these reclusive apes. She became the first scientist to see orangutans mate and give birth. She was the first to observe a fight between adult males. She was also the first to discover that male orangutans do occasionally sleep on the ground rather than in the trees.

11 By recording everything she observed, Birute Galdikas greatly advanced human understanding of these primates. She discovered that female orangutans have their first baby at age 16 and care for that baby for eight years before having another offspring, giving them the longest birth interval of any wild animal. She documented 400 different food items orangutans eat. And she learned that although these apes are basically solitary creatures, they do engage in subtle forms of social interaction.

12 By the 1980s, Birute was the world's leading expert on orangutans. By then, she was also a leader in the fight to protect these elusive creatures. There are only about 50,000 wild orangutans left in the world. With humans encroaching on their turf, their fate seems uncertain. Birute has worked hard to save what natural habitat they have left.

13 In 1997, after more than 25 years in the jungles, Birute Galdikas won the prestigious Tyler Prize. This prize is awarded for outstanding achievements in environmental studies. Birute has racked up several other awards, as well. She has been named Indonesia's "Hero for the Earth." She has been honored in Canada, England, and the United States. She has medals and awards from a dozen different agencies. For her, though, the greatest reward does not come from humans. It comes from working with the orangutans themselves. "When I look into the eyes of an orangutan," she says, "I see God."

If you have been timed while reading this article, enter your reading time below. Then turn to the Words-per-Minute Table on page 195 and look up your reading speed (words per minute). Enter your reading speed on the graph on page 196.

Reading Time: Lesson 21

_____ : _____
Minutes   Seconds

A Finding the Main Idea

One statement below expresses the main idea of the article. One statement is too general, or too broad. The other statement explains only part of the article; it is too narrow. Label the statements using the following key:

M—Main Idea   **B—Too Broad**   **N—Too Narrow**

_____ 1. Birute Galdikas had learned many facts about orangutans, including what they eat, how they mate, and where they sleep.

_____ 2. Expanding the realm of human knowledge is a worthwhile undertaking.

_____ 3. With tremendous determination, scientist Birute Galdikas learned details about the orangutan that no one had ever known before.

_____ Score 15 points for a correct M answer.

_____ Score 5 points for each correct B or N answer.

_____ **Total Score:** Finding the Main Idea

B Recalling Facts

How well do you remember the facts in the article? Put an X in the box next to the answer that correctly completes each statement about the article.

1. Birute Galdikas grew up in
☐ a. the United States.
☐ b. Borneo.
☐ c. Canada.

2. Galdikas was inspired to study orangutans by
☐ a. Louis Leakey.
☐ b. Jane Goodall.
☐ c. Dian Fossey.

3. While looking for orangutans, Galdikas came down with
☐ a. bubonic plague.
☐ b. pneumonia.
☐ c. dengue fever.

4. Birute was the first scientist to observe male orangutans
☐ a. eating.
☐ b. fighting.
☐ c. sleeping.

5. Birute Galdikas won the
☐ a. Tyler Prize for environmental studies.
☐ b. Nobel Prize for biology.
☐ c. Presidential Medal of Freedom.

_____ Score 5 points for each correct answer.

_____ **Total Score:** Recalling Facts

C | Making Inferences

When you combine your own experience and information from a text to draw a conclusion that is not directly stated in that text, you are making an inference. Below are five statements that may or may not be inferences based on information in the article. Label the statements using the following key:

C—Correct Inference   F—Faulty Inference

_____ 1. Only women are suited for studying primates in the wild.

_____ 2. Birute Galdikas has become quite wealthy because her studies of orangutans.

_____ 3. Once you get malaria, you have it off and on for many years.

_____ 4. Orangutans are tolerant of humans who follow them around but cause them no trouble.

_____ 5. Birute Galdikas feels both respect and affection for orangutans.

Score 5 points for each correct answer.

_____ **Total Score:** Making Inferences

D | Using Words Precisely

Each numbered sentence below contains an underlined word or phrase from the article. Following the sentence are three definitions. One definition is closest to the meaning of the underlined word. One definition is opposite or nearly opposite. Label those two definitions using the following key. Do not label the remaining definition.

C—Closest   O—Opposite or Nearly Opposite

1. She also suffered severe skin burns after sitting down on a log that oozed <u>toxic</u> sap.

_____ a. healthy

_____ b. stinging

_____ c. poisonous

2. She <u>doggedly</u> followed orangutans through miles of dense jungle.

_____ a. stubbornly

_____ b. lazily

_____ c. angrily

3. She compiled book after book of records detailing the behavior of these <u>reclusive</u> apes.

_____ a. endangered

_____ b. sociable

_____ c. solitary

4. With humans <u>encroaching on</u> their turf, their fate seems uncertain.

_____ a. avoiding

_____ b. intruding upon

_____ c. flying over

5. In 1997, after more than 25 years in the jungles, Birute Galdikas won the <u>prestigious</u> Tyler Prize.

_____ a. famous and respected

_____ b. profitable

_____ c. little-known

_____ Score 3 points for each correct C answer.

_____ Score 2 points for each correct O answer.

_____ **Total Score:** Using Words Precisely

Enter the four total scores in the spaces below, and add them together to find your Reading Comprehension Score. Then record your score on the graph on page 197.

Score	Question Type	Lesson 21
_____	Finding the Main Idea	
_____	Recalling Facts	
_____	Making Inferences	
_____	Using Words Precisely	
_____	**Reading Comprehension Score**	

Author's Approach

Put an X in the box next to the correct answer.

1. The author uses the first paragraph of the article to

☐ a. inform the reader about Galdikas's job.

☐ b. describe the setting through which Galdikas and her husband were traveling.

☐ c. compare Birute Galdikas and her husband.

2. What is the author's purpose in writing "Studying the Secret Lives of Orangutans"?

☐ a. To encourage the reader to study orangutans

☐ b. To inform the reader about a dedicated scientist

☐ c. To express an opinion about saving the orangutan

3. From the statements below, choose those that you believe the author would agree with.

☐ a. Birute Galdikas shows unusual dedication to her profession.

☐ b. People should try to save orangutans from extinction.

☐ c. Birute Galdikas has wasted her life by living with orangutans in the jungle.

4. How is the author's purpose for writing the article expressed in paragraph 11?

☐ a. The author repeats the fact that orangutans are solitary creatures.

☐ b. The author claims that Galdikas has greatly advanced human understanding of orangutans.

☐ c. The author lists many facts about orangutans.

_____ Number of correct answers

Record your personal assessment of your work on the Critical Thinking Chart on page 198.

CRITICAL THINKING

Summarizing and Paraphrasing

Follow the directions provided for question 1. Put an X in the box next to the correct answer for question 2.

1. Complete the following one-sentence summary of the article using the lettered phrases from the phrase bank below. Write the letters on the lines.

Phrase Bank:

a. Galdikas's first trip into the jungle

b. Galdikas's awards and her opinion of orangutans

c. how Galdikas has observed orangutans

The article about Birute Galdikas begins with _____, goes on to explain _____, and ends with _____.

2. Read the statement about the article below. Then read the paraphrase of that statement. Choose the reason that best tells why the paraphrase does not say the same thing as the statement.

Statement: Galdikas is concerned that humans are invading the orangutan habitat.

Paraphrase: For many years, Galdikas has worked to protect the orangutan from encroaching humans who build their highways, towns, and factories too close to the orangutan's habitat.

☐ a.   Paraphrase says too much.

☐ b.   Paraphrase doesn't say enough.

☐ c.   Paraphrase doesn't agree with the statement about the article.

_____ Number of correct answers

Record your personal assessment of your work on the Critical Thinking Chart on page 198.

Critical Thinking

Put an X in the box next to the correct answer for questions 1 and 4. Follow the directions provided for the other questions.

1. From what Birute Galdikas said, you can predict that she will

☐ a.   discourage anyone else from studying the orangutan.

☐ b.   leave orangutan research up to younger scientists from now on.

☐ c.   continue to study the orangutan.

2. Choose from the letters below to correctly complete the following statement. Write the letters on the lines.

In the article, _____ and _____ are alike in their willingness to spend their lives studying primates.

a.   Birute Galdikas

b.   Louis Leakey

c.   Jane Goodall

3. Read paragraph 8. Then choose from the letters below to correctly complete the following statement. Write the letters on the lines.

According to paragraph 8, _____ because _____.

a.   Birute suffered severe skin burns

b.   Birute spent a great deal of time in swamp water

c.   Birute developed ulcerous sores on her legs

4. How is the story of Birute Galdikas related to the theme of this book?

☐ a. Galdikas discovered facts that no one had ever known before.

☐ b. Galdikas persevered in her research in spite of great difficulties.

☐ c. Galdikas received a number of awards for her work.

_____ Number of correct answers

Record your personal assessment of your work on the Critical Thinking Chart on page 198.

Personal Response

I know how Birute Galdikas feels about the animals she studies because

_____

_____

_____

_____

Self-Assessment

One of the things I did best when reading this article was

_____

_____

_____

I believe I did this well because

_____

_____

_____

_____

CRITICAL THINKING

Compare and Contrast

Think about the articles you have read in Unit Three. Choose the four individuals you admire the most. Write the titles of the articles about them in the first column of the chart below. Use information you learned from the articles to fill in the empty boxes in the chart.

Title	What difficulties did this person have to overcome?	What three adjectives would describe this person best?	How did this person benefit from his or her invention or discovery?

If I could meet one of these individuals, I would choose _____. I would ask this question: _____

_____

_____

Words-per-Minute Table

Unit Three

Directions: If you were timed while reading an article, refer to the Reading Time you recorded in the box at the end of the article. Use this words-per-minute table to determine your reading speed for that article. Then plot your reading speed on the graph on page 196.

Lesson / No. of Words	15 / 1063	16 / 1087	17 / 1240	18 / 1197	19 / 1034	20 / 1162	21 / 1119	Seconds
1:30	709	725	827	798	689	775	746	90
1:40	638	652	744	718	620	697	671	100
1:50	580	593	676	653	564	634	610	110
2:00	532	544	620	599	517	581	560	120
2:10	491	502	572	552	477	536	516	130
2:20	456	466	531	513	443	498	480	140
2:30	425	435	496	479	414	465	448	150
2:40	399	408	465	449	388	436	420	160
2:50	375	384	438	422	365	410	395	170
3:00	354	362	413	399	345	387	373	180
3:10	336	343	392	378	327	367	353	190
3:20	319	326	372	359	310	349	336	200
3:30	304	311	354	342	295	332	320	210
3:40	290	296	338	326	282	317	305	220
3:50	277	284	323	312	270	303	292	230
4:00	266	272	310	299	259	291	280	240
4:10	255	261	298	287	248	279	269	250
4:20	245	251	286	276	239	268	258	260
4:30	236	242	276	266	230	258	249	270
4:40	228	233	266	257	222	249	240	280
4:50	220	225	257	248	214	240	232	290
5:00	213	217	248	239	207	232	224	300
5:10	206	210	240	232	200	225	217	310
5:20	199	204	233	224	194	218	210	320
5:30	193	198	225	218	188	211	203	330
5:40	188	192	219	211	182	205	197	340
5:50	182	186	213	205	177	199	192	350
6:00	177	181	207	200	172	194	187	360
6:10	172	176	201	194	168	188	181	370
6:20	168	172	196	189	163	183	177	380
6:30	164	167	191	184	159	179	172	390
6:40	159	163	186	180	155	174	168	400
6:50	156	159	181	175	151	170	164	410
7:00	152	155	177	171	148	166	160	420
7:10	148	152	173	167	144	162	156	430
7:20	145	148	169	163	141	158	153	440
7:30	142	145	165	160	138	155	149	450
7:40	139	142	162	156	135	152	146	460
7:50	136	139	158	153	132	148	143	470
8:00	133	136	155	150	129	145	140	480

Minutes and Seconds

Plotting Your Progress: Reading Speed

Unit Three

Directions: If you were timed while reading an article, write your words-per-minute rate for that in the box under the number of the lesson. Then plot your reading speed on the graph by putting a small X on the line directly above the number of the lesson, across from the number of words per minute you read. As you mark your speed for each lesson, graph your progress by drawing a line to connect the X's.

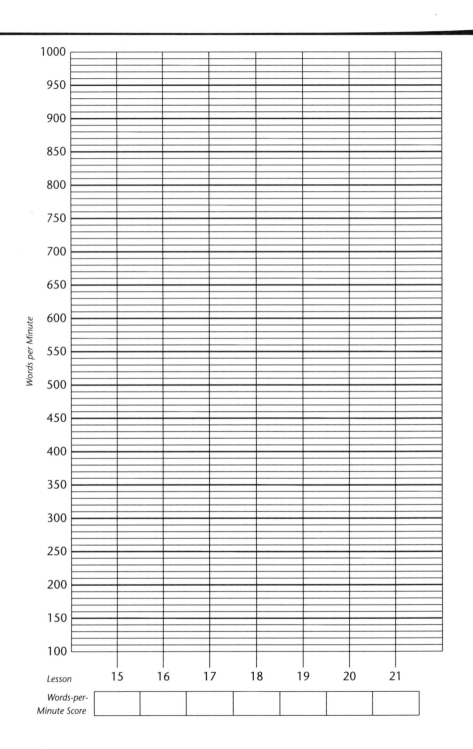

Plotting Your Progress: Reading Comprehension

Unit Three

Directions: Write your Reading Comprehension score for each lesson in the box under the number of the lesson. Then plot your score on the graph by putting a small X on the line directly above the number of the lesson and across from the score you earned. As you mark your score for each lesson, graph your progress by drawing a line to connect the X's.

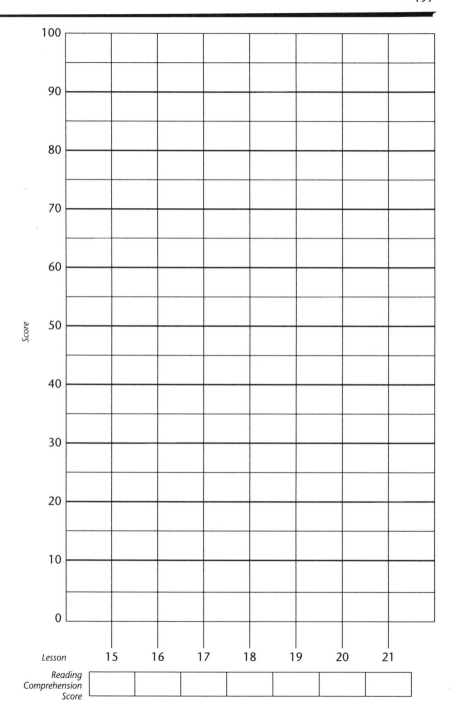

Score

Lesson   15   16   17   18   19   20   21

Reading
Comprehension
Score

Plotting Your Progress: Critical Thinking

Unit Three

Directions: Work with your teacher to evaluate your responses to the Critical Thinking questions for each lesson. Then fill in the appropriate spaces in the chart below. For each lesson and each type of Critical Thinking question, do the following: Mark a minus sign (–) in the box to indicate areas in which you feel you could improve. Mark a plus sign (+) to indicate areas in which you feel you did well. Mark a minus-slash-plus sign (–/+) to indicate areas in which you had mixed success. Then write any comments you have about your performance, including ideas for improvement.

Lesson	Author's Approach	Summarizing and Paraphrasing	Critical Thinking
15			
16			
17			
18			
19			
20			
21			

Picture Credits

Cover: Photo montage by Karen Christoffersen

Sample Lesson: pp. 3, 4 Corbis-Bettmann; p. 5 The Granger Collection

Unit 1 Opener: p. 13 Corbis-Bettmann

Lesson 1 p. 14 Corbis-Bettmann; p. 15 The Granger Collection

Lesson 2 p. 22 The Granger Collection; p. 23 UPI/Corbis-Bettmann

Lesson 3 p. 30 Archive Photos; p. 31 UPI/Corbis-Bettmann

Lesson 4 p. 38 © Kevin Schafer/Peter Arnold, Inc.; p. 39 The Granger Collection

Lesson 5 p. 46 Corbis-Bettmann; p. 47 The Granger Collection

Lesson 6 p. 54 © Brooks Kraft/Sygma; p. 55 © Gamma-Liaison

Lesson 7 p. 54 © Wendy Stone/Gamma Liaison; p. 55 Corbis-Bettmann

Unit 2 Opener p. 75 Wolfgang Kaehler/Liaison International

Lesson 8 p. 76 © Steven Frankel/Photo Researchers; Inset: © Wolfgang Kaehler/Liaison International; p. 77 © Daniel Zirinsky/Photo Researchers, Inc.

Lesson 9 pp. 84, 85 Courtesy The Gillette Company

Lesson 10 p. 92 © Richard Weiss/Peter Arnold, Inc.; p. 93 National Geographic Image Collection

Lesson 11 p. 100 The Kobal Collection; p. 101 Archive Photos

Lesson 12 p. 108 © North Wind Pictures; p. 109 Corbis-Bettmann

Lesson 13 pp. 116, 117 © Richard T. Nowitz

Lesson 14 p. 124 © Pat Clyne; p. 125 © Susan Greenwood/Gamma Liaison

Unit 3 Opener p. 137 John Reader/Science Photo Library/Photo Researchers

Lesson 15 p. 138 Hulton Getty/Gamma-Liaison; p. 139 © Lee Boltin

Lesson 16 p. 146 Maximilian Stock/Science Photo Library; p. 147 Archive Photos

Lesson 17 p. 154 Corbis-Bettmann; p. 155 The Bancroft Library/UC, Berkeley

Lesson 18 p. 162 Corbis-Bettmann; p. 163 © Chris Bjornberg/Photo Researchers, Inc.

Lesson 19 p. 170 John Reader/Science Photo Library/Photo Researchers; p. 171 UPI/Corbis-Bettmann

Lesson 20 p. 178 Corbis-Bettmann; Inset: © Emory Kristof/National Geographic Image Collection; p. 179 Archive Photos

Lesson 21 p. 186 © Orangutan Foundation